FINDING OUT ABOUT

Medical Research

Dr Martin Hughes

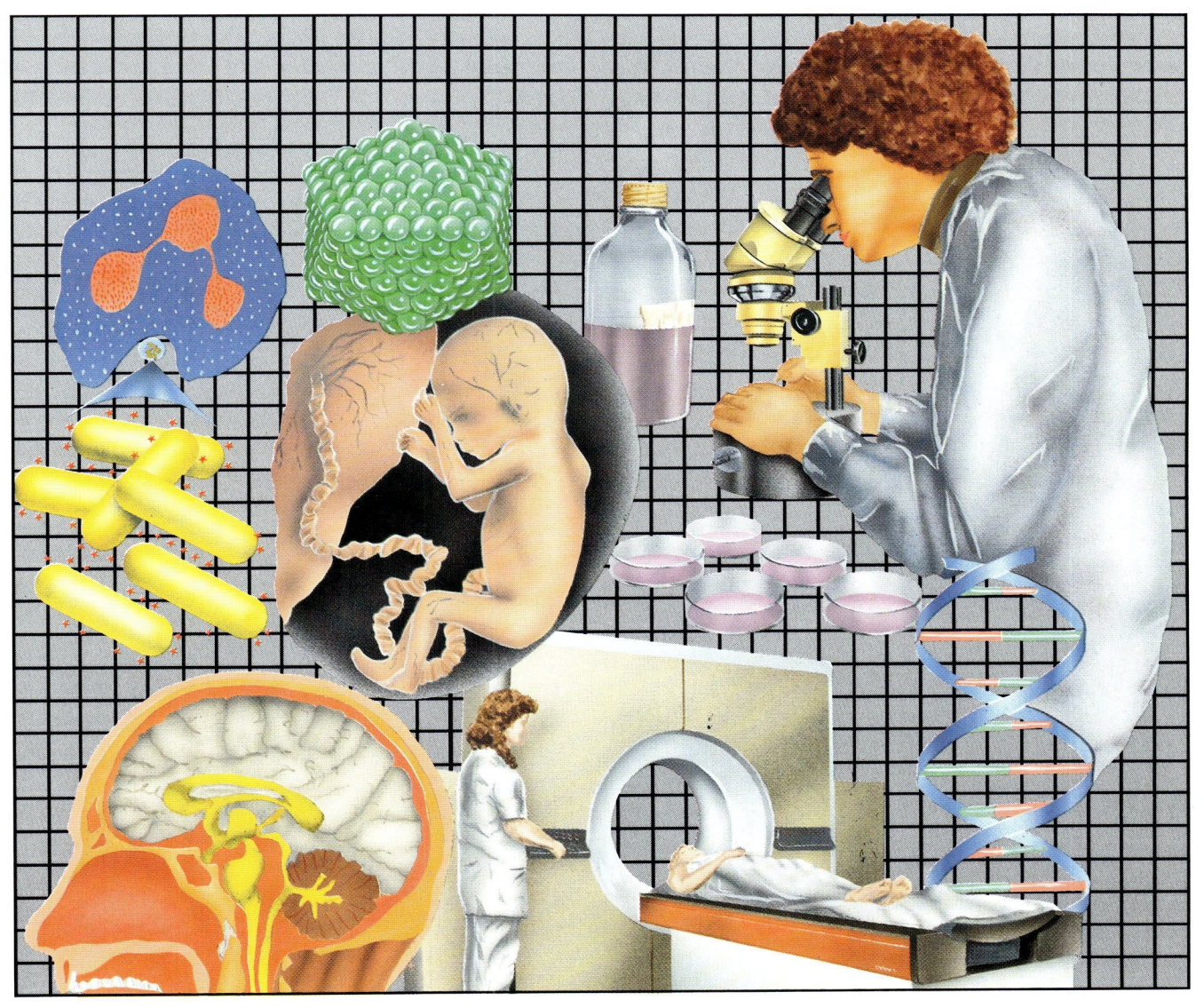

FRANKLIN WATTS
LONDON • NEW YORK • SYDNEY • TORONTO

Contents

This edition published 1990 by
Franklin Watts
96 Leonard Street
London EC2A 4RH

ISBN 0 7496 0328 3

Original edition published 1988 by
Hobsons Publishing plc
Produced in conjunction with and sponsored by
the Medical Research Council and the
Wellcome Trust

Copyright © 1988 Hobsons Publishing plc

A CIP catalogue record for this book is
available from the British Library

1 Some questions to start

Why do you think that thousands of people used to die of **polio**, but nowadays, in the developed world, it is rare?

Why is it that there used to be lots of children with painful deformed limbs, but nowadays there are few?

As people get older, the lens in the eye – the part that we look through just behind the pupil – gets cloudier. Sometimes it clouds over completely and we can no longer see through it. This used to mean blindness, but now it doesn't. Why?

Other parts of the body are also affected by 'wear and tear'. This used to mean that many elderly patients could not move without severe pain; now they can move with ease. Why is that?

Antibiotics are chemicals which we use to treat many infectious diseases; one of the best known antibiotics is **penicillin**. In the 1940s it cost thousands of pounds to treat a single patient with a course of penicillin but today it costs only a pound or two. Why?

What is medical research?

We have just had a series of questions about some illnesses which used to cause suffering, but which we can now control. *Research* can be thought of as looking for answers to problems: it means asking questions, and more questions, until we have the answers – or literally re-searching. We've found answers to many of the problems but there are still a lot of questions to be answered.

Let's see how research works with a disease like **acne**.

First, we need to identify the problem; then we need to find the cause. Knowing the cause helps us to develop a treatment – either by removing the cause or by treating the effects.

With acne the problem is easy to identify, since it is obvious at a glance. Most teenagers have spots which they find embarrassing (and so do some adults). Girls may find that their spottiness varies according to the stage of their menstrual cycle. Examining the affected skin under the microscope shows that the cause of the problem involves the tiny glands which supply the lubrication (called sebum) to the hairs growing on our body. The glands can get blocked; they become infected and then inflamed, which produces angry spots.

We have established the cause; can we produce a treatment? We can't reduce the number of ducts, because we're born with them; but we can reduce the degree of blockage, the number of microbes, or the amount of sebum (this is dependent on a male hormone called *testosterone*, which is why boys often have more acne than girls).

Other diseases are more difficult to identify than acne, but the principle is the same: recognising the pattern of disease amongst a group of people or across a country or over a period of time helps to identify the problem.

Developing a treatment

The aim of treatment is to reduce ill health. This often means developing an effective medicine, or a **vaccine**. Many medicines were discovered by chance.

In 1928 Alexander Fleming, doing experiments involving the growing of germs, noticed that on one of his experiments the germ – a **bacterium** – did not grow where some mould had already begun to grow. By closer examination the active substance penicillin was found. That discovery has saved millions of lives. We will discuss penicillin in more detail on page 5.

Alexander Fleming who discovered penicillin. He won the Nobel prize in 1945.

WHAT YOU CAN DO

Find out what you can about Alexander Fleming. Can you think of any other famous scientists who have made important discoveries in the medical field?

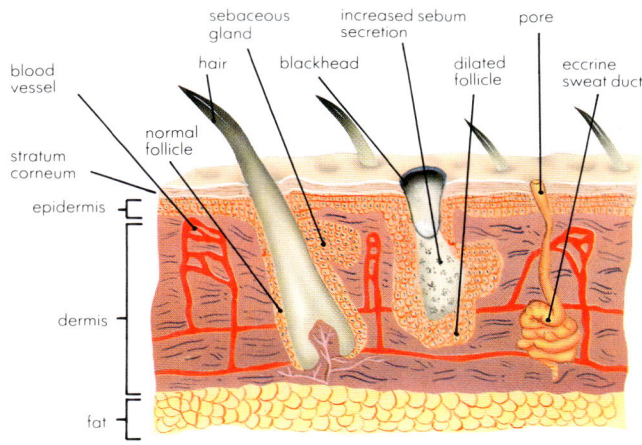

Cross-section through skin

blood vessel — stratum corneum — normal follicle — hair — sebaceous gland — blackhead — increased sebum secretion — dilated follicle — pore — eccrine sweat duct — epidermis — dermis — fat

An **infectious** disease is one which we get when our bodies are infected or invaded by another species called a **micro-organism**. There are a number of different types, each type having many different members. We commonly call them 'germs'.

They are called 'micro-organisms' because they are small, much smaller than the naked eye can see, but have independent structures which together allow some form of life. Some are more complex than others.

Bacteria are among the largest, but are still minute organisms. If we were to take one of the larger types, and measure it, the distance end to end would be about 20 microns (a micron is a millionth of a metre). To put it another way, you would need about 11,000 to measure a centimetre. Many are much smaller.

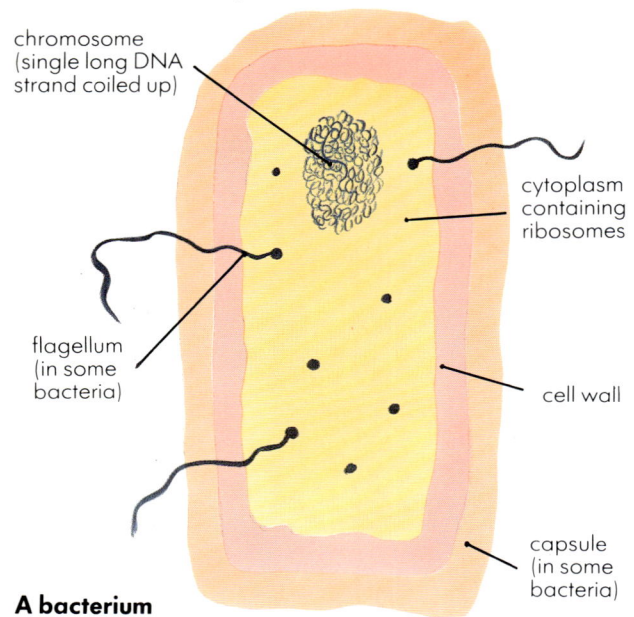

chromosome
(single long DNA
strand coiled up)

cytoplasm
containing
ribosomes

flagellum
(in some
bacteria)

cell wall

capsule
(in some
bacteria)

A bacterium

They are of different shapes, small and round, long and thin, corkscrew-shaped, and so have different names.

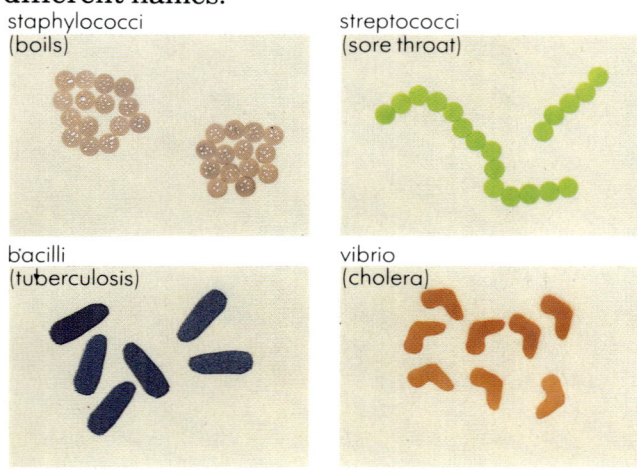

staphylococci
(boils)

streptococci
(sore throat)

bacilli
(tuberculosis)

vibrio
(cholera)

As members of the plant kingdom, they reproduce by a process of fission, or splitting. One cell splits to become two, and so on. In the course of a day, a single bacterium may develop into 16 million bacteria.

Not all bacteria are harmful to us. In fact, we depend on them for many processes, such as the digestion of food, but some cause life-threatening illnesses such as **tuberculosis** (TB).

Tuberculosis was once common in this country. It is carried by a bacterium which measures 4 microns in length, and is less than 1 micron wide. We can be infected either by inhaling droplets coughed or sneezed by an infected person or (much more rarely) by drinking milk from an infected animal. Once inhaled (or ingested), the bacterium multiplies and may be spread to many different parts of the body.

In the developed world, there has been a dramatic drop in the number of cases of TB since the end of the Second World War.

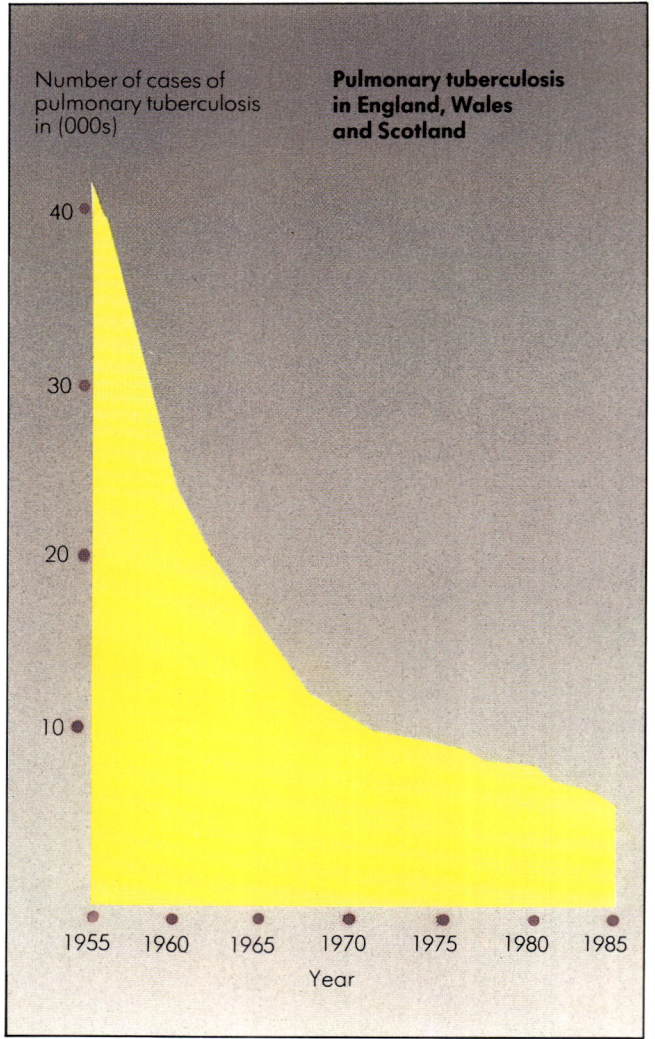

Number of cases of
pulmonary tuberculosis
in (000s)

**Pulmonary tuberculosis
in England, Wales
and Scotland**

40

30

20

10

1955 1960 1965 1970 1975 1980 1985
Year

You can see that nowadays the disease in this country has become relatively uncommon.

Why has the disease become rarer? There are a number of reasons:

First – the cause has been identified and we now have tests to establish who has it.

Second – we have developed effective treatments to cure the disease, so there are fewer infectious cases spreading it.

Third – the general state of health and nutrition in this country has improved, so that resistance is better.

Fourth – we can vaccinate (see page 23) people to protect them from developing the disease if they are exposed to it.

Fifth – the bacterium has been virtually eradicated from cows: all milk drunk in this country should be free from TB.

How do we know which micro-organisms cause which diseases, and how do we know how to treat them?

The study of micro-organisms is called *microbiology*. Microbiologists are skilled at investigating samples from people with infectious disease, and finding the germ responsible; *biochemists* are experts in the study of the chemistry of living cells; and *pharmacologists* are scientists who apply their knowledge of chemicals and medicines to problems that may arise in living systems.

The isolation of penicillin by Sir Alexander Fleming from the mould was the start of the study of chemicals called antibiotics. These are used to treat bacterial infections.

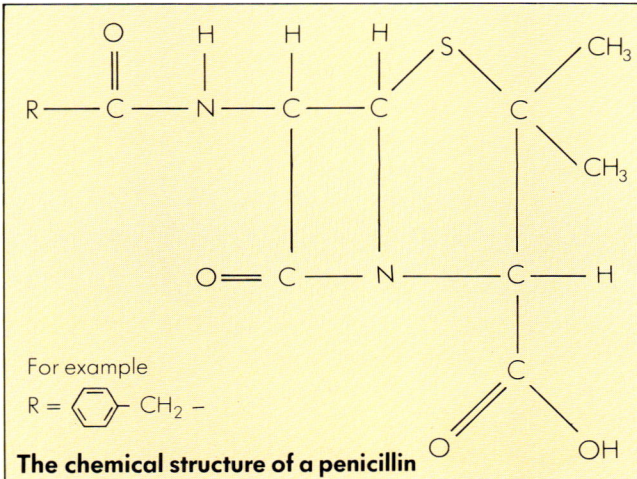

The chemical structure of a penicillin

The penicillins interfere with the formation of the **cell wall** in the dividing bacteria: if the bacteria have no cell wall, they die.

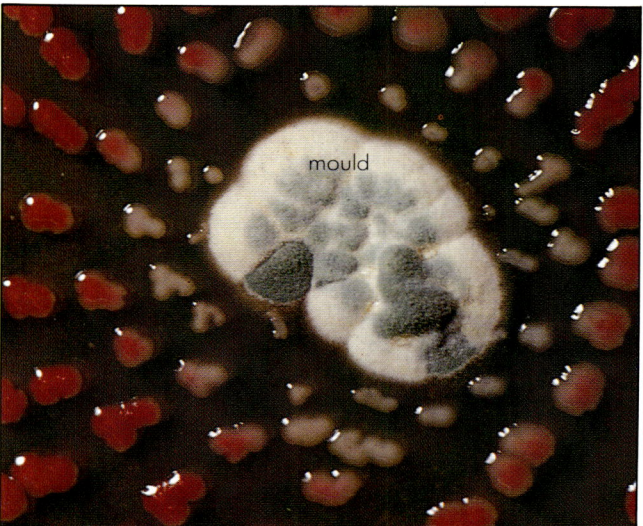

The bacteria do not grow in the area where there is mould (penicillium).

Penicillins are active against many bacteria, such as those which cause diseases from tonsillitis to pneumonia, and many others. By developing techniques to produce large amounts of penicillin, pharmaceutical companies have greatly reduced the cost of the medicine.

Some bacteria, however, do not respond to penicillin, either because the cell wall is not susceptible or because they produce a chemical which destroys the penicillin.

Diseases caused by these bacteria – such as some skin infections – will not respond to ordinary penicillin. Researchers have therefore discovered and developed more antibiotics which are effective against many 'resistant' organisms. Some of these antibiotics act like penicillin but have a slightly different structure. Others act entirely differently by preventing the bacteria from reproducing.

Although we now have these powerful medicines to stop many bacterial infections, many others are difficult to treat, either because the bacteria change their structure or because we haven't yet developed a successful antibiotic. Let's hope the research develops new antibiotics faster than the bacteria develop resistance!

NOW TRY THESE

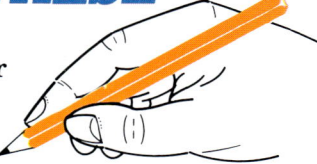

1 Why is penicillin now much cheaper than when it was first introduced?

2 Why was it necessary for researchers to develop other antibiotics besides penicillin?

3 How has research helped to stop viral infections?

We have seen how some infectious diseases are caused by bacteria – which are very small – and how we can treat them. There are very much smaller micro-organisms called **viruses**. They are responsible for some of the most lethal diseases. Viruses cause rabies, Lassa fever, AIDS and many other serious illnesses, and some cancers, as well as mild diseases like the common cold or the simple wart. As with bacteria, there are a number of different types, with differing structures.

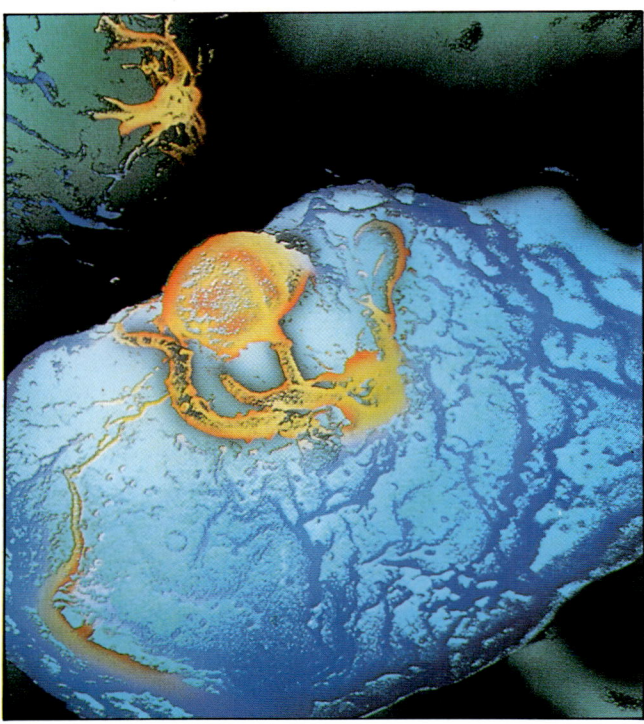

Electron microscope view of the AIDS virus growing in a human white cell.

However, all viruses have certain features in common. They are much simpler than bacteria, since basically they consist only of a strand of genetic material and a covering. They do not contain the protein-making machinery – the 'ribosomes'.

Cross-section through a virus

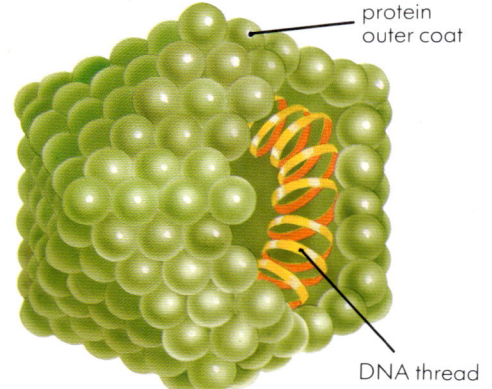

protein outer coat

DNA thread

This type of virus is responsible for diseases like chicken pox.

In order to reproduce itself, the virus needs to borrow the machinery it doesn't have – the ribosomes. It finds these in the cells of the **host** – the plant, animal, or human it has infected.

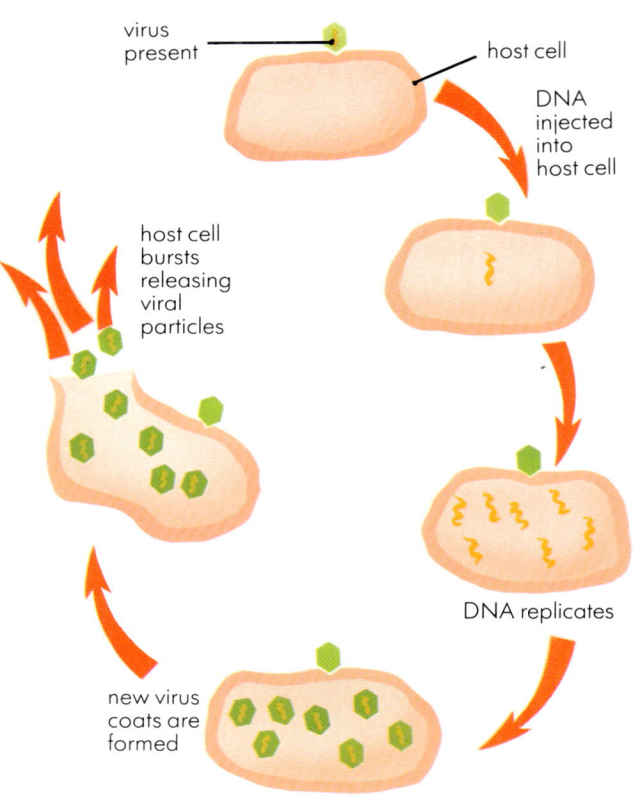

virus present

host cell

DNA injected into host cell

host cell bursts releasing viral particles

DNA replicates

new virus coats are formed

The virus is simply a strand of genetic material: its aim is to reproduce itself.

One virus enters a cell. Inside the cell it sheds its cover and its genetic material is fed into the ribosomes. Very shortly the 'host' cell is filled with virus particles, the cell dies and the viruses are released to infect other cells. Very quickly one virus particle can become millions.

How do we examine viruses?

Viruses are so small that, even when magnified 60 times, the biggest still measures only 1/100 of a millimetre – so we can't see them with ordinary microscopes. By research, we have developed electron microscopes which use beams of electrons rather than beams of light.

These can magnify many hundreds of thousands of times, so we can 'see' the tiny viruses in the cells.

Other research has enabled us to grow viruses in the laboratory and so examine the molecular structure of each type of virus so that we know what sort of genetic material it contains and what the cover is made of.

How do we know who's infected?

Viruses are small, but the things they infect – such as human beings – are much bigger. Our bodies have 'defence systems' (described on page 20) which respond to an attack by an infectious micro-organism. This response includes the production of chemicals called **antibodies** designed to inactivate the virus. We can now measure the amounts of antibody in any patient by doing blood tests: since different viruses cause the production of different antibodies, we can find which virus has infected the patient. (This is how the AIDS test works.)

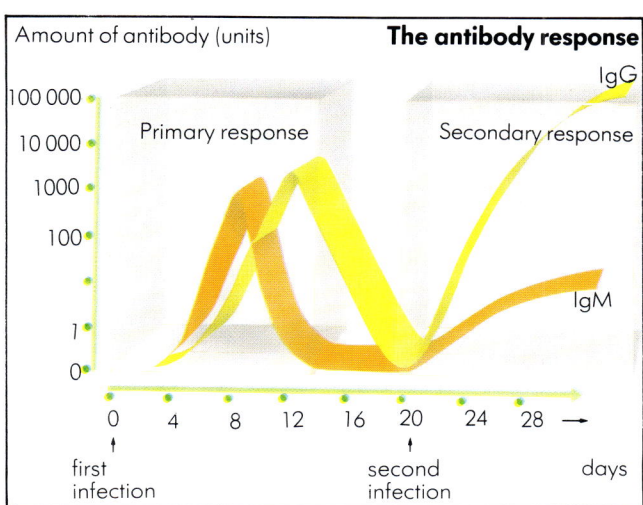

The antibodies are produced in response to an infection. The level stays high until all the viruses have been inactivated, and then drops. The next time we are infected, the body responds more quickly.

We can identify the virus, and the patient it has infected – how does this help? Since viruses live inside the cells they infect, we cannot attack them using antibiotics. There are as yet very few treatments available for viral infections – mostly we have to wait until the body's defences drive the virus away.

There is one family of viruses – the **Herpes** family – which causes several infections, including the simple cold sore and chicken-pox. This can re-emerge years later as shingles. The herpes virus can lie *dormant*, hiding away until for some reason it becomes active and reproduces, causing illness.

There is now a medicine (Acyclovir) made by Wellcome which can stop the herpes virus reproducing and is useful in preventing the symptoms, provided it is started early enough. But the major means of fighting viral illness at the present time is by using **immunisation** (page 23) to prevent such infections occurring, or by using some of the body's own defence chemicals (the antibodies) to stop infection developing.

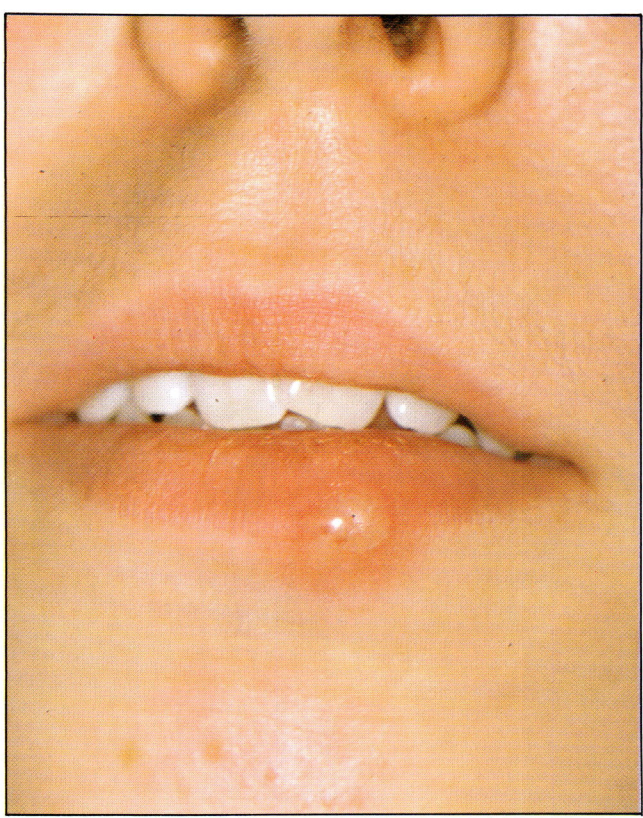

A cold sore – caused by Herpes simplex – can return many times.

Much research still needs to be done, however, before we have effective treatments for many viral illnesses. So far the first steps – isolation and identification – are the only parts of the research process which have been generally successful.

NOW TRY THESE

1 What are the differences between a bacterium and a virus?

2 How do viruses reproduce themselves in the body?

3 What are antibodies? Why does the body make antibodies?

4 Name at least three diseases caused by a virus.

5 Why are virus infections so difficult to treat?

6 At present, what is the major means of fighting viral infections?

7 What are the most recent developments enabling us to stop the spread of AIDS?

How has research helped to stop other parasitic infections?

A **parasite** is an organism which depends on another for the necessities of life.

Malaria is an unpleasant disease causing fever, headache, shaking, possible failure of the kidneys and brain, and sometimes death. It is present in most of the tropical areas of the world and is caused by the introduction of a parasite. The infection arises through a bite from an infected mosquito.

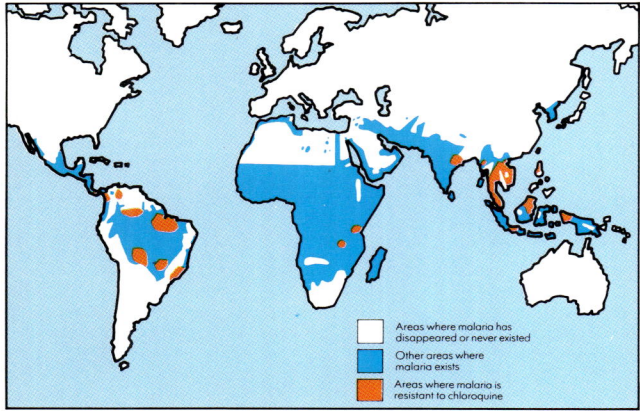

Key:
- Areas where malaria has disappeared or never existed
- Other areas where malaria exists
- Areas where malaria is resistant to chloroquine

Map showing the distribution of malaria.

For malaria to spread, there must be both infected mosquitoes and human beings: the parasite needs both to develop fully. In the human, the parasites develop **asexually** in the liver and the red blood cells. Some then mature to become 'sexual' forms. These cannot develop further in the human – they need the mosquito.

In the mosquito, the sexual forms develop further and progress to the salivary glands, from which they infect the next human the mosquito bites, so that the whole cycle starts again.

Mosquitoes breed in marshy areas and shallow water: drainage of the marshes and use of insecticides have got rid of some mosquitoes. Better results have been obtained by treatment of infected people with medicines: adequate treatment will remove all the infective sexual forms.

It's better, of course, not to become infected. We can stop travellers catching malaria when they visit an area where they might be bitten by an infected mosquito by making sure they are already taking the anti-malarial medicines.

Unfortunately, malarial parasites in various parts of the world are becoming resistant to the medicines available; research is needed to develop new medicines so that we can continue to control the spread of malaria.

Researchers have identified other parasitic infections, and studied the ways in which they are spread to humans. Many – such as the illness called **elephantiasis** caused by a small roundworm – only occur in tropical areas and are frequently spread by mosquitoes or other insects.

Another worm, spread by the bite of a midge, affects over 30 million people in the tropical rain forests. Many of these people will become blind

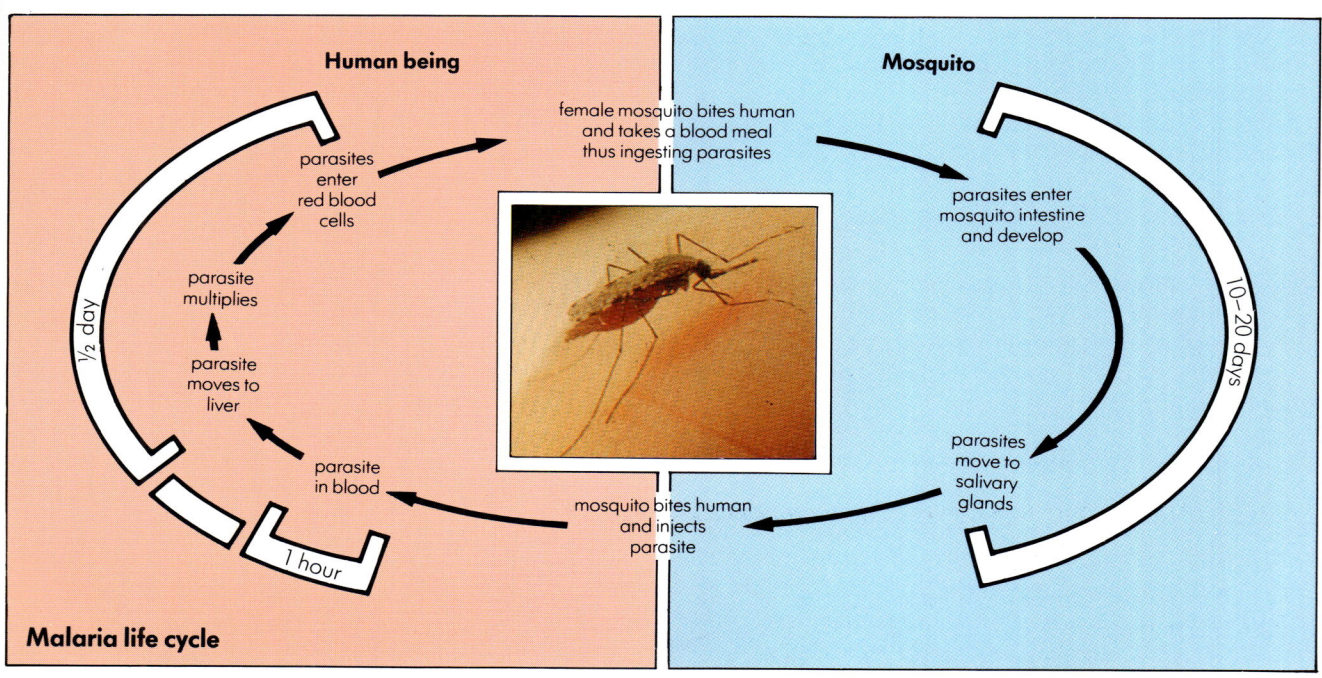

Human being

parasites enter red blood cells

parasite multiplies

parasite moves to liver

parasite in blood

½ day

1 hour

female mosquito bites human and takes a blood meal thus ingesting parasites

Mosquito

parasites enter mosquito intestine and develop

parasites move to salivary glands

10–20 days

mosquito bites human and injects parasite

Malaria life cycle

Part of the cycle takes place in the human, and part in the mosquito. The disease passes from person to person via the mosquito.

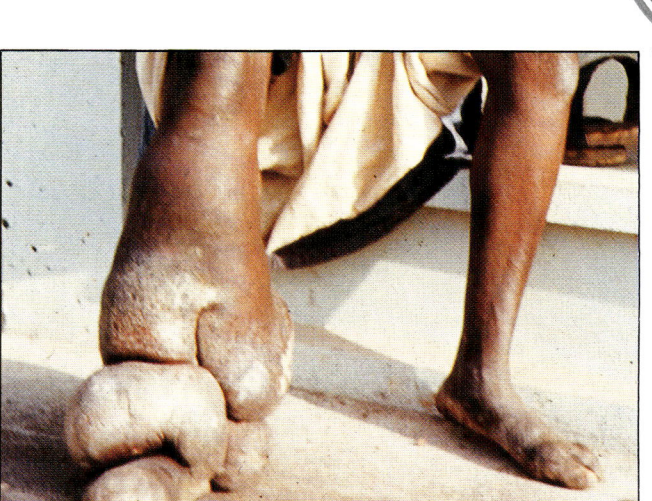

The small worm develops and blocks the tiny vessels which drain the lymphatic fluid from our legs. The legs can become very big and painful. You can see why it's called Elephantiasis.

as a result of damage caused to their eyes by the worm. This is called *'river blindness'*.

As with malaria, both the above diseases can be reduced by treatment of the infected person, reducing the area available for the breeding of the insect that carries the parasite, and by measures to avoid the bite (like using mosquito nets).

Not all parasites carried by insects occur in tropical regions alone. The **louse** is a blood-sucking insect which can infest human beings. There are two different types – the head louse and the body louse. Both of these exist throughout the world. They cannot exist away from the human being and can be spread by personal contact. They lay their eggs (called nits) which become attached to hairs or clothes, and feed by piercing the skin and sucking blood.

It's not just the louse that is a parasite: it can pass on its own parasite as well.

Body lice, unlike head lice, flourish in overcrowded and dirty conditions. Their bites cause itching and scratching – but far more unpleasant is the infection they may carry. Some lice are infected by a micro-organism

which causes a disease called **typhus** in man. Every year, there are cases of typhus all over the world.

As we have seen with other types of infectious disease, the way to control the problem is to prevent infection – by insecticides, improved hygiene and reduction of overcrowded conditions. If the disease does occur, we must treat the infected person to remove the parasite – with typhus, we can use antibiotics.

Throughout history, millions of people have suffered and died as a result of great **epidemics**. We now know, from descriptions in history books and from other studies, that of these the following were the worst:

smallpox and *yellow fever* were caused by viruses;

plague and *cholera* were caused by bacteria;

and the fifth, *typhus*, by a micro-organism carried by parasites.

Today smallpox has been eradicated throughout the world by immunisation; yellow fever is preventable by immunisation; plague (see page 22) has been removed from the developed world by improved hygiene and the control of rats – any cases that occur can be treated; cholera can be prevented by purifying water supplies, immunising people at risk, and treating any cases that occur; and typhus can be prevented by improved hygiene and treatment of any established cases.

These no longer pose any real threat; they have been tamed by medical research. There are, however, other diseases to which we must pay attention . . . can you think of any?

NOW TRY THESE

1 How is malaria spread?

2 In what parts of the world is the malarial mosquito found?

3 What is the most effective way of preventing the spread of malaria?

4 How can yellow fever be prevented?

5 What is the key factor in preventing plague, typhus and cholera?

5 Cancer: how has research helped?

What is cancer? From the beginning, all living things grow. Every living thing starts as one single cell. The cell divides and divides and changes until development stops. This is normal growth.

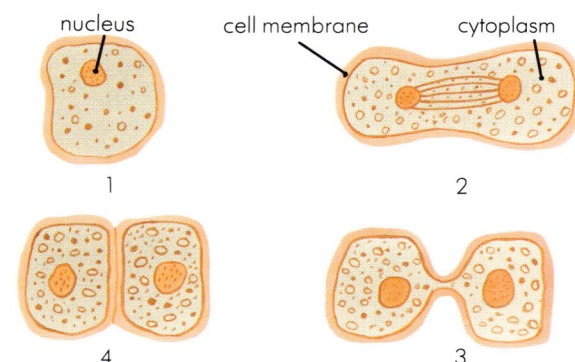

We start off as one cell. This divides and produces more, and so on until the whole human being or animal is produced.

A simple cell, like an *amoeba*, produces more amoebae. A more complicated cell – like a plant cell – produces a plant. All the cells in the plant or the animal initially came from the same cell, yet in the end they may be very different: rose thorns are not the same as rose petals, just as our noses are not the same as our knees.

This is an amoeba. It is a single-cell animal that can cause bowel disease.

We are not sure how or why cells change as they develop; the process is called **differentiation** and means that cells change into different things. We know what is happening, but we don't know why. Normally, cells change and develop as they are supposed to, and then stop when they reach the correct size. We don't know why they stop – our tongues don't grow until they fill our heads; our bones don't grow through our skin. The problem with cancers is that they don't stop.

A cancer comes from cells that change when they shouldn't, grow when they shouldn't, and go where they shouldn't. This means that the cancer patient has too many of the wrong cells in the wrong place. The danger here is that the wrong types of cell in the wrong places can cause pain and interfere with the normal function of affected parts of the body: this is how cancers kill.

In human beings, most cells continue to divide throughout life, to replace cells that are lost

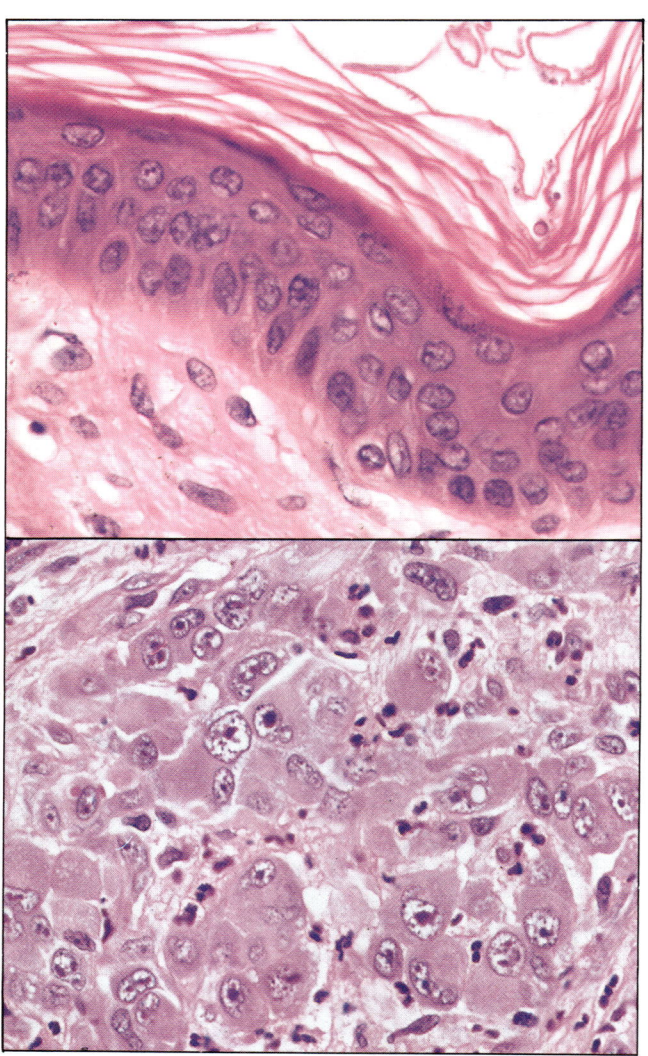

The top picture shows normal skin; the bottom one shows a type of skin cancer where the abnormal cells are much less ordered and are dividing more quickly.

through wear and tear or injury. Some – like skin cells and blood cells – are replaced more quickly than others, like nerve cells (which grow very slowly). The cells with the fastest replacement become malignant (malignant is another word for cancerous) more often. Cancer can attack many different parts of the body, eg the skin, lungs, intestines and so on.

Can cancers be stopped?

Fifty years ago, the answer was most often 'no'. Nowadays quite often the answer is 'yes' – though some can be stopped more easily than others.

Skin cancer

Normal skin has a number of layers. The cells on the surface are constantly being replaced. Sometimes the cells change, and become cancerous or malignant, producing a skin cancer.

The treatment is straightforward: the whole area can be removed, or the cancer can be destroyed either by radiation or heat treatment.

Skin cancer is becoming more common. It occurs much more frequently in Australia, or in white-skinned people who have spent many years in Africa. It is much more likely to occur on some parts of the body than others, and Australians get it more often on their right arms, while Americans get it more often on their left. Can you think of a reason why?

Leukaemia – another type of cancer

'Leukaemia' means literally that the blood 'turns white'. Normal blood consists mainly of red blood cells, with a few white cells which form part of the body's defences (described on page 20). These are called leukocytes. If the white cells turn cancerous, and grow faster, the red cells get swamped and the body can't function. The blood looks white.

Patients – who may be young children – become very weak, and bruise very easily.

Researchers have developed treatments that cure many cases of leukaemia. We can use blood transfusions to replace the red blood cells that have been overwhelmed by the cancerous white cells. Once we have done this, and the patient is stronger, we can inactivate the abnormal white cells using special medicines and X-rays.

As a result of these developments, *90% of cases of some types of leukaemia can be cured*. What was once nearly always a fatal disease is now in many cases a treatable illness.

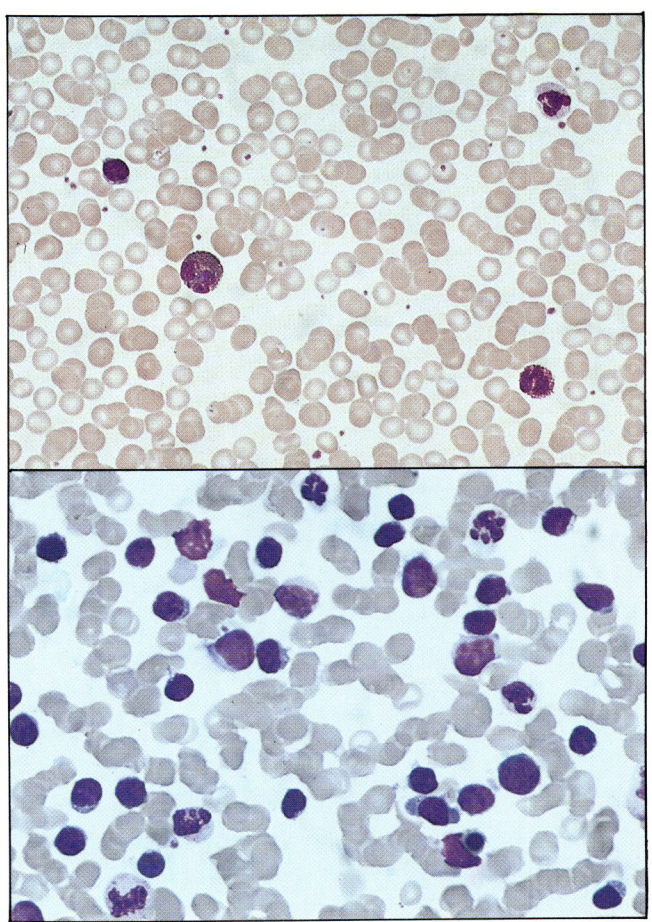

Normal blood – at the top – contains only a few white cells (which look blue under the microscope). In a case of leukaemia – at the bottom – there are far too many.

The people who treat cancers have great success in dealing with those such as the two described above. Other cancers can also be cured – by medicines, radiotherapy, surgery, or a combination of all three.

NOW TRY THESE

1 How does a cancer cell differ from a normal cell?

2 Name some types of cell in the body which are replaced more quickly than others.

3 Which type of cancer is becoming more common, and why?

4 Name some ways in which cancer can be treated.

5 What does the word 'leukaemia' mean?

6 What is radiotherapy?

Cancer: causes and consequences

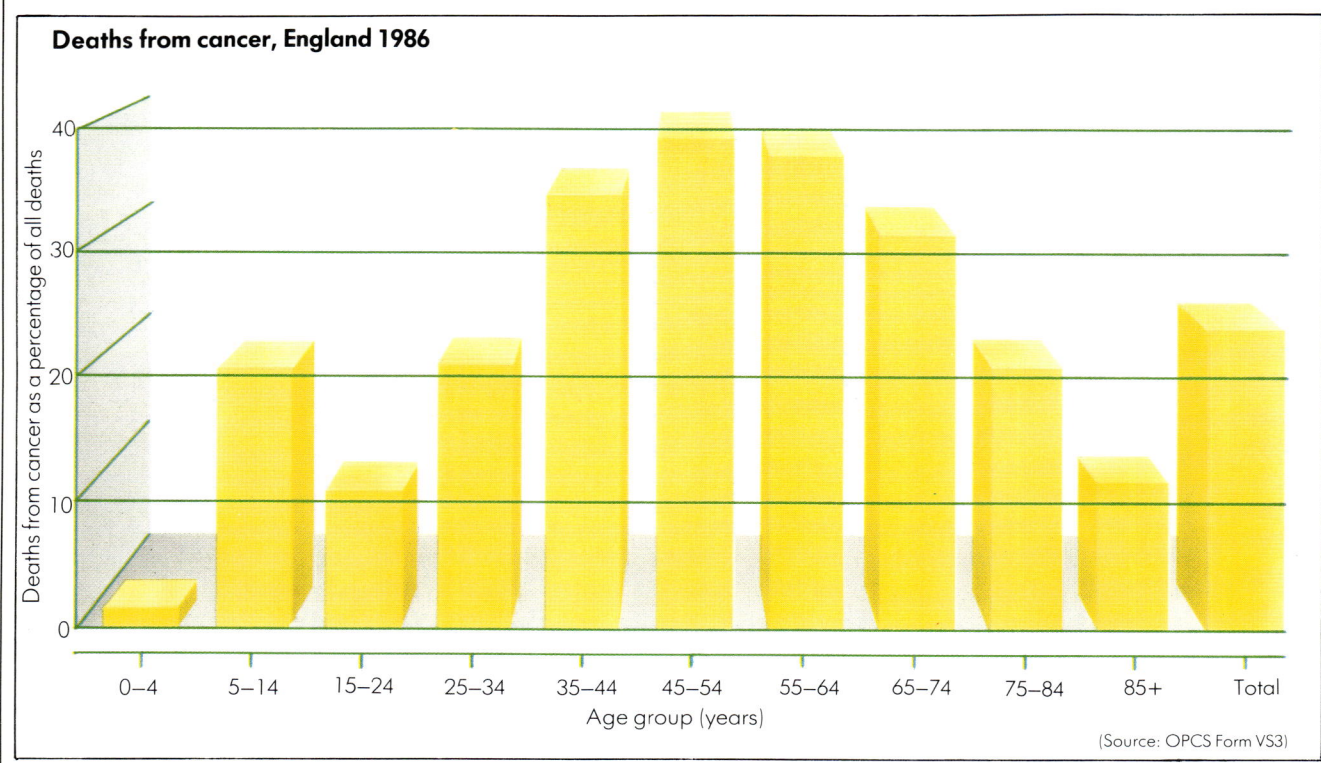

Deaths from cancer, England 1986

Deaths from cancer as a percentage of all deaths

Age group (years)

0–4 5–14 15–24 25–34 35–44 45–54 55–64 65–74 75–84 85+ Total

(Source: OPCS Form VS3)

You can see from the graph above that many people die each year from cancer. Up to one-third of the population may be affected.

Why do we get it?

If we can find out why things happen, we may be able to stop them. Research has helped us to find out many causes of cancer.

Most cases of lung cancer are caused by cigarette smoking. We have found this by comparing the

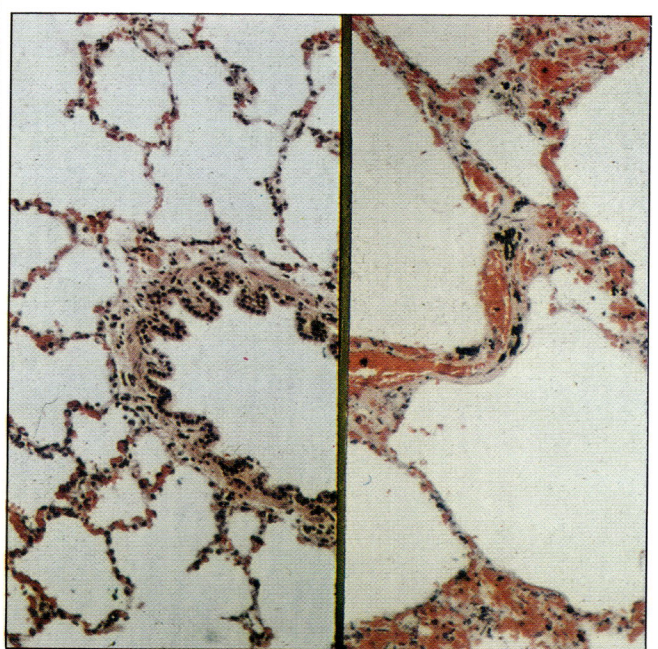

Lung tissue is delicate: exposing it to irritant smoke causes irreversible damage.

smoking habits of people with lung cancer with those people who do not have it. Smoking, particularly heavy smoking, is far more common among people with lung cancer.

CIGARETTE SMOKE CAUSES LUNG CANCER

This sort of research, studying numbers and comparing rates of illness, helps us to identify causes. We need experiments to help us to understand how such causes produce the illness. We have seen that cancers start when cells grow and change unexpectedly. Cancers can also start when cells grow too quickly because they are damaged. Our lungs are lined with cells very similar to the cells on our skin.

With skin cancer, the damage is not from smoke, but from sunlight. Sunlight is good for us; it is necessary to make things grow. However, too much sunlight can make some skin cells grow abnormally: this is one reason why there is more skin cancer in Australia than in Britain, and in white-skinned people in Africa for example.

Many of us travel abroad to the sunshine more frequently than we used to: we are exposed more often to the effects of the sun's rays. As a result, more of us are developing skin cancers. The cancers, as we have seen, can be dealt with, but it's better if we take precautions to prevent the cancer from starting. With lung cancer, the answer is not to smoke. With skin cancer, we have to protect the skin from the effects of the sun.

Sun-barrier creams help to protect us from developing skin cancer.

We have cells in our skin which produce a pigment – melanin – responsible for the colour of our hair and skin.

As with all cells, the melanin-producing cells can grow out of control, and become malignant.

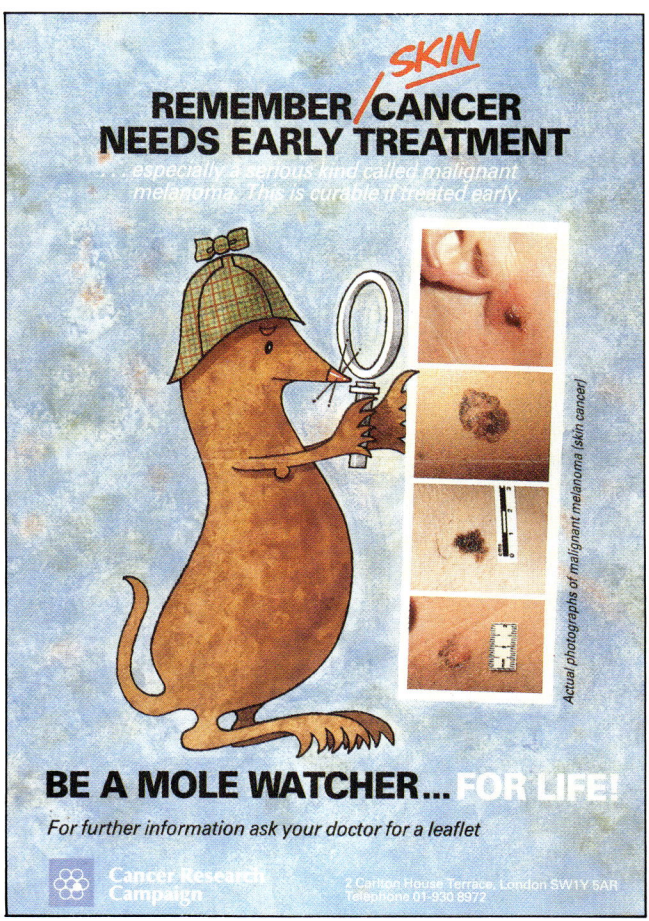

This is a dangerous cancer, called a melanoma. Unlike some skin cancers, this can spread and be very difficult to treat. We can cure it if we remove the abnormal cells at an *early* stage, before there has been any spread. This is true of most cancers: early detection and early treatment mean early cure.

Cancer of the intestine

We can see the skin: we can't see the cells lining the intestine. Like skin cells and blood cells, these divide frequently: as a result, they sometimes become cancerous. We know from research that the chance of the cancer spreading to other parts of the body depends on how long it has been present. Again, if we find these cancerous cells early, we can cure them by removing them.

How can we find them, if we can't 'see' the intestine?

By studying many cases of bowel cancer, we know that it starts as a growth of cells that stand out from the wall of the intestine – a 'polyp'. This can be removed quite easily if we know it's there. By studying the 'family history' of people who might be at risk from bowel cancer, we should be able to detect cases early and stop them developing. If all people at risk were tested early, the disease would kill far less frequently.

The same is true of most other cancers: we can treat some once they have developed, but often the only hope is in early detection. Research is aimed at developing treatment where we can, but better results come from finding cases before treatment is hopeless. This means knowing who might be 'at risk' from the environment and their jobs (page 24), or from their family history, as well as from their habits, like smoking.

NOW TRY THESE

1 How harmful is cigarette smoking to a person's health?

2 What evidence is there regarding the effects of cigarette smoking?

3 What other factors can cause cancer?

4 How would you protect your skin from the sun?

5 How could some types of cancer be prevented?

13

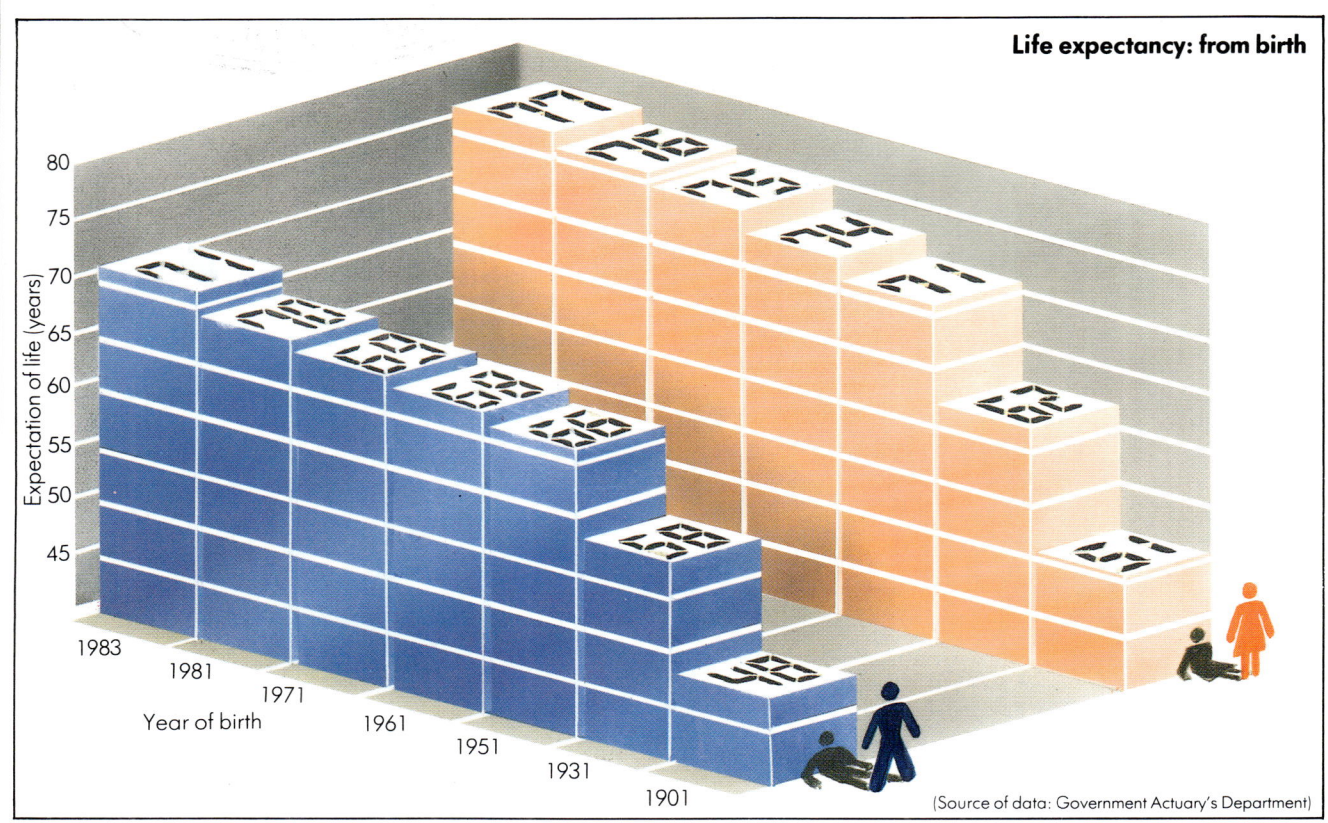

Life expectancy: from birth

Expectation of life (years)

80
75
70
65
60
55
50
45

1983
1981
1971
1961
1951
1931
1901

Year of birth

(Source of data: Government Actuary's Department)

Our expected length of life increases year by year. Can you think of any reasons why?

No living thing lasts forever. Butterflies live for days only, while some trees may last centuries, but in the end all living things die.

In the time of Henry VIII, a man was considered old if he reached the age of 40. Today, we expect to live almost twice as long as that.

One of the consequences of this is that our bodies have longer to develop the changes associated with long use – they begin to show signs of 'wear and tear'.

Our skin becomes less tight as we get older: we develop wrinkles. Our joints ache and become stiffer as a consequence of decades of movement. Our bones – particularly if we are female – become more brittle; our spines may get shorter as the bones shrink; our vision gets worse – we need stronger glasses; we feel the cold because our arteries get stiffer and may become blocked, so the circulation is poor: all these are events that may happen to each of us as we grow old.

When wear and tear produces pain or disability, we need to intervene. Research has provided solutions to many of the problems: for example, stiffness and pain in the joints can literally be a crippling condition.

It is called osteo-arthritis of the joints and it gets worse as time goes on.

We don't know why the *cartilage* which lines the joint breaks up more in some people than in others. We know that if the joint is subjected to unusual stresses or strains – either because there has been previous damage, such as a fracture, or because the load it carries is excessive (because its owner is overweight), the damage develops much more quickly. In the early stages, we can prevent the symptoms by using medicines which interfere with our ability to feel pain. The damage is still present, but we don't feel it.

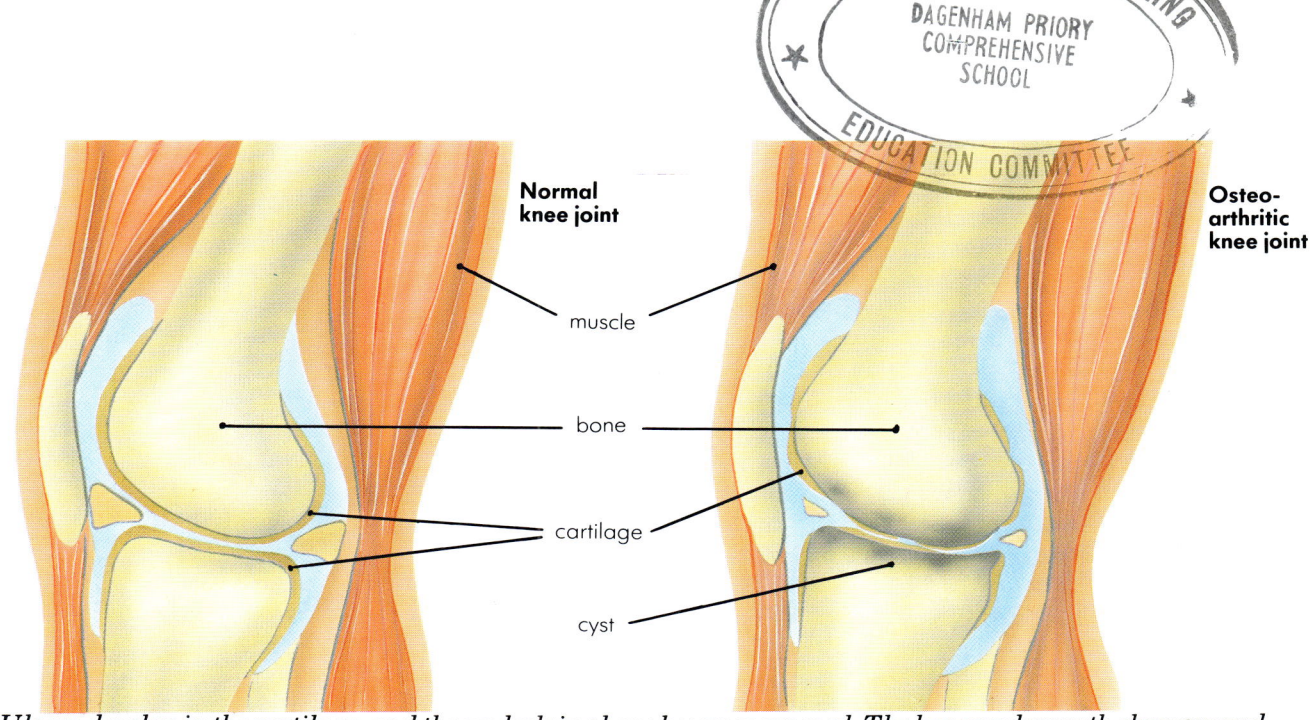

Normal knee joint

Osteo-arthritic knee joint

muscle

bone

cartilage

cyst

Ulcers develop in the cartilage, and the underlying bone becomes exposed. The bone underneath changes and cysts can appear.

When these medicines no longer provide relief, or when the stiffness becomes so great that it becomes impossible to walk even short distances, we can replace the joints. Scientists and surgeons together developed effective replacement parts for the hip, in the 1950s. Today, many thousands of replacement operations are performed every year.

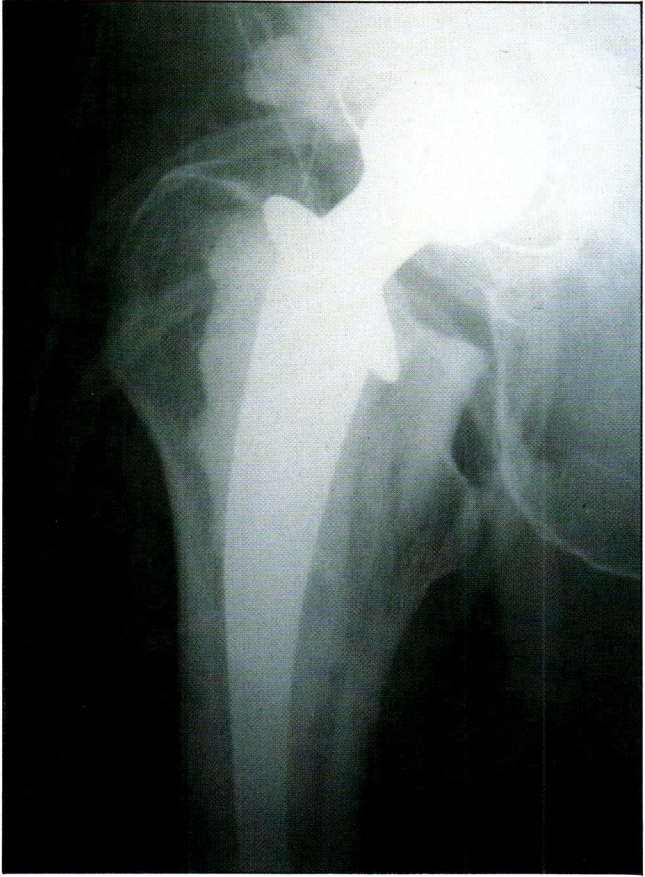

In this patient, the worn hip joint has been removed and replaced with a metal one.

With increasing age, all parts of our bodies suffer damage to a greater or lesser extent. The eye contains a transparent lens which changes shape as we look from a near object to a distant one.

With age, the lens becomes cloudy, possibly owing to the amount of light it has been exposed to. The cloudiness can progress until the lens is opaque: the patient may only be able to see the vaguest movement with the affected eye. This is a **cataract** – in some parts of the world, it is a very common cause of blindness. We have developed ways to remove the lens, and replace it either with a lens inside the eye, or with a contact lens, so that vision can be restored.

We have considered only a very few instances of bodily 'wear and tear' where medical research has provided a solution. There are many others: there are other joints that surgeons can replace; there are other medicines to help other illnesses, because all parts of the body are subject to wear and tear. Can you think of any other conditions that become more common as we get older?

NOW TRY THESE

1 Describe some of the changes that occur in our bodies as we grow older.

2 Find out what kinds of replacement parts have been developed for the body.

3 Describe the eye condition known as a cataract.

Disease affecting the brain

It is not only the body that is affected by wear and tear: the brain too is made up of cells – millions of them – that can fail to function, or function at the wrong time, or function too much. The brain controls our movements, our speech, our behaviour and even our thoughts and feelings; any of these can be affected.

The cells of the brain 'talk' to each other by tiny electrical charges or by sending 'chemical messages' using quite simple molecules. Because these molecules transmit messages, they are called 'transmitters'. Many thousands of such messages are carried every second.

The brain receives information about the outside world via the electrical messages carried by the nerves that supply our five senses (what are they?). It instructs us to move or take other action in response to the information it receives. The movements we make are usually controlled and precise: most of us can close our eyes and touch our noses with our fingers.

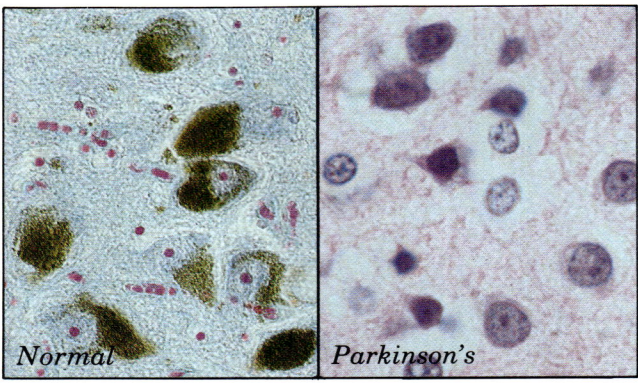

Normal   *Parkinson's*

In the patient with Parkinson's disease, the dark nerve fibres are pale: there is a reduction in a chemical transmitter.

Many disorders can affect our movements: in **Parkinson's Disease**, there is too much movement of the hands and too little movement of the rest of the body: the limbs are stiff, while the hands may tremble continuously, as if the patient is agitated. The illness is due to an imbalance of some of the transmitters in certain cells in the middle of the brain.

Patients with this disease – which affects 1% of people over 60 – used to be confined to wheelchairs. By finding the cause, we have been able to develop ways of replacing the missing transmitter, and easing the symptoms. Research is now aimed at preventing the disease from developing and finding ways to repair the damaged cells.

Epilepsy is another disorder of movement. Instead of the cells in the brain sending signals or messages to each other in an ordered way, a group of cells sends a large number of signals. In

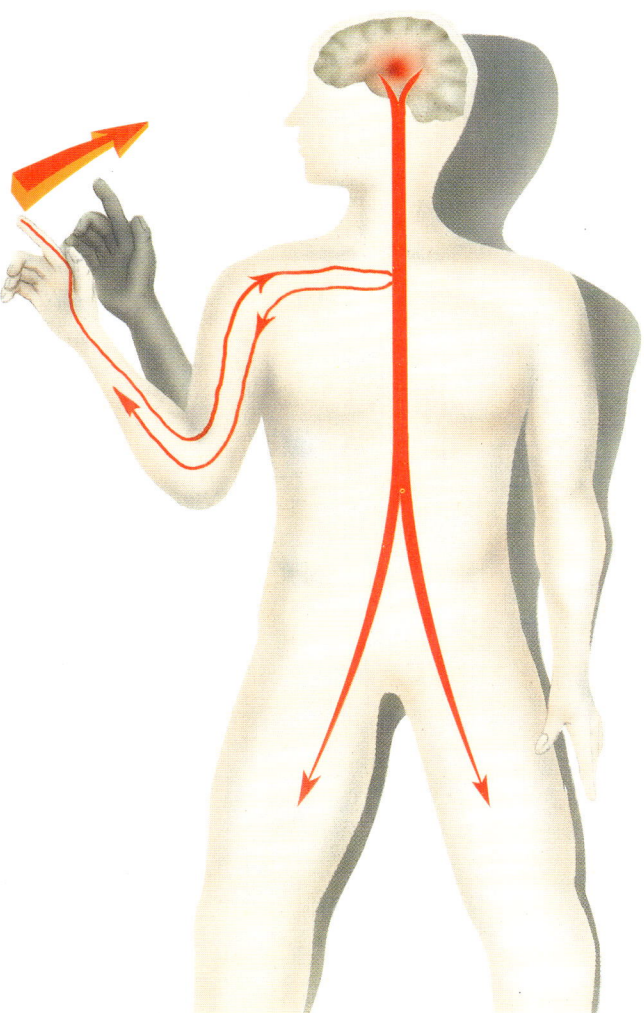

Information is carried to the sensory area of the brain which communicates with the motor area and may produce a 'reflex' movement of the body.

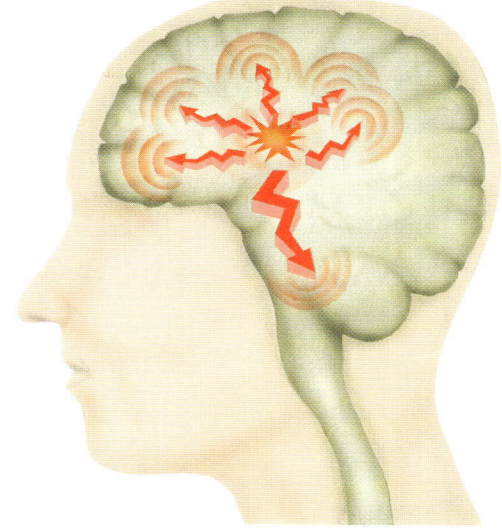

Epilepsy – when something triggers the abnormal cells, the activity spreads to affect neighbouring cells. We can trace the electrical activity in the brain which can help us to find the cause.

some people this causes lots of cells to respond all at once: there may be repeated movements of the part of the body controlled by those cells – an arm or a leg or sometimes the whole body. We refer to this as a *'fit'* or a *'convulsion'*. Often the patient becomes unconscious.

There are many causes of epilepsy such as infections or head injuries, but with most people who have it the cause is not clear. It seems that some of us are more likely than others to develop abnormal electrical activity in the brain. Research has been directed towards preventing fits in these people; we now have many effective medicines which can allow epileptics to lead normal lives.

Epilepsy can affect any age group, though it is less common in the middle decades of life. Very young children may have fits when their temperature rises as a result of infection: some of these children go on to develop epilepsy as adults. Fits become more common after the age of 50 as a result of a decrease in blood supply to the brain cells.

The general process of ageing also affects the brain cells. The brain shrinks. One effect of this shrinkage is that, as we age, our memories fade, and our fingers are not as nimble as they were. These are normal changes. Some people are affected to a much greater degree – they become muddled and confused, they are unable to care for themselves, they lose control of their bodies and become incontinent, they no longer recognise their families or friends. Eventually, they become rigid and immobile, and die. This disease is called dementia, which means 'without mind', and is a disorder of thought, behaviour and movement. In the UK it affects 5% of people over the age of 65, and 10% of those over 80. One type of dementia is Alzheimer's disease which affects over half a million people in the UK.

How can research help? There is as yet no way to prevent dementia. We need first to find the cause.

We can examine brain cells under the microscope. By identifying the abnormalities and combining the information with biochemical studies, it might be possible to find the chemical problem underlying the disorder, and then develop a treatment.

Disorders of thought and behaviour are not confined to the elderly. Any person at any age may develop an illness affecting the mind rather than the body. Such mental illnesses are just as much a disease as polio or pneumonia, and can cause just as much suffering. One of these – **schizophrenia** – occurs most often between the ages of 25 and 30. Because sufferers often appear to have thoughts and feelings that are not their own, it was once thought that this was due to a 'split mind'. It is a very distressing disorder which affects many people, some of them for many years.

We now know that this disease runs in families, and it is likely that it arises because of a defect in the system that relays messages between different parts of the brain. Many of the terrifying symptoms of schizophrenia can be alleviated by using medicines. Since the disease can affect patients' memories and therefore their reliability in taking medication, ways have been developed of producing 'depots' or stores of the medicine in patients. These can last weeks before needing replacement.

As a result, many patients who would previously have been locked away in hospitals can now lead useful lives. As we come to understand more about the chemical activity of the brain, and its control, we shall understand more of the nature of mental illness, and be better able to help sufferers. This is the aim of research.

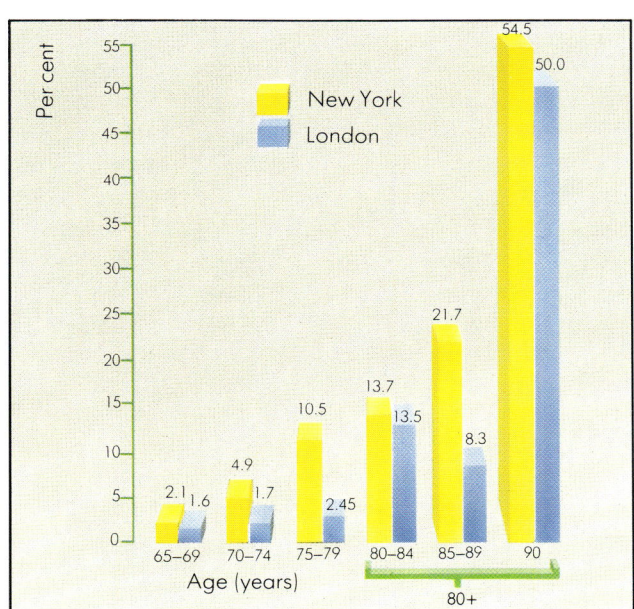

Distribution of dementia cases by age in New York and London.

NOW TRY THESE

1 What is dementia?

2 In your own words, describe the disease schizophrenia.

Heart disease: the Western killer

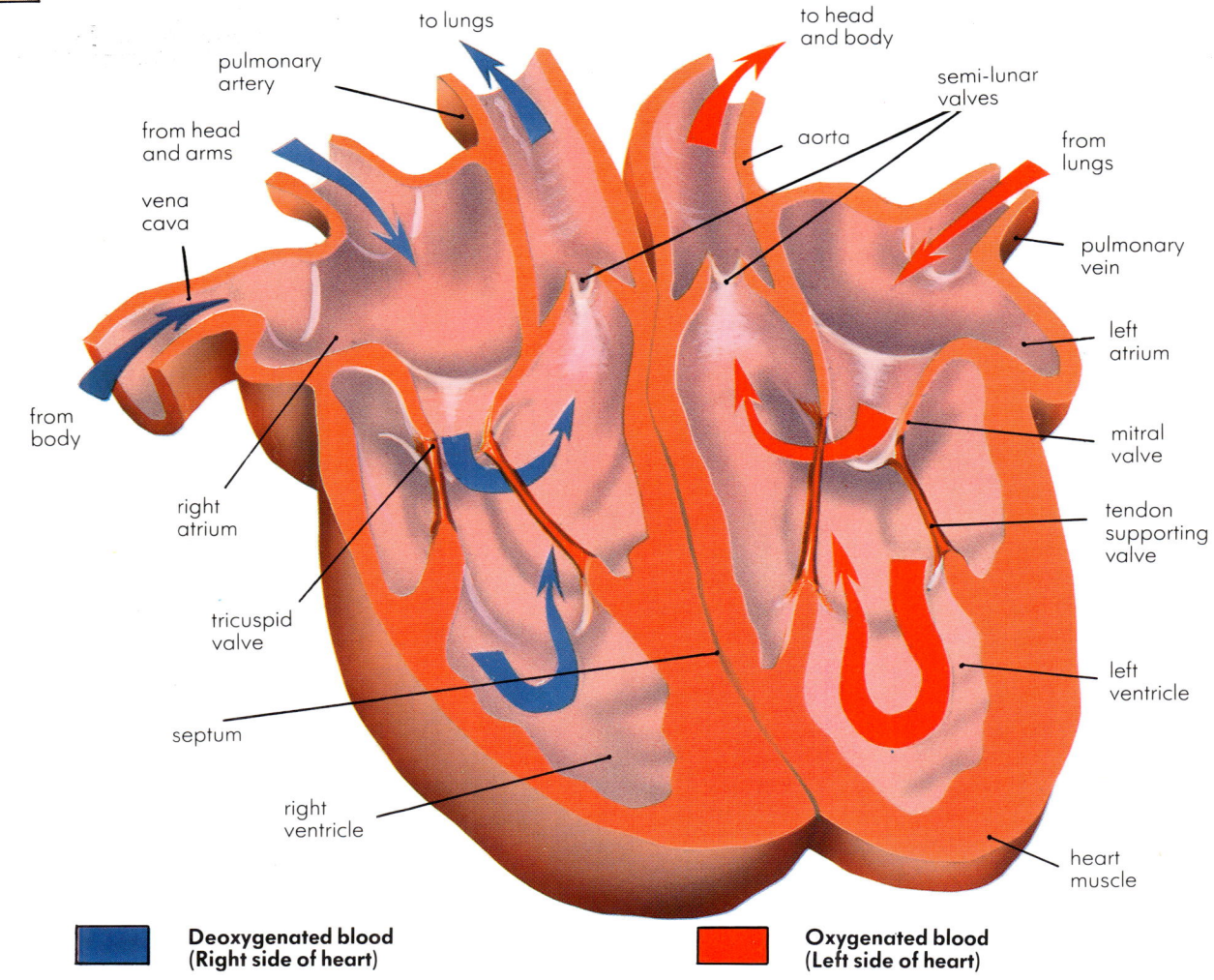

to lungs

pulmonary
artery

from head
and arms

vena
cava

from
body

right
atrium

tricuspid
valve

septum

right
ventricle

to head
and body

semi-lunar
valves

aorta

from
lungs

pulmonary
vein

left
atrium

mitral
valve

tendon
supporting
valve

left
ventricle

heart
muscle

Deoxygenated blood
(Right side of heart)

Oxygenated blood
(Left side of heart)

Vertical section through a human heart

The right side of the heart receives blood from the veins, and pumps it to the lungs; the left side receives blood saturated with oxygen from the lungs, and pumps it round the body.

Many more people die today from heart disease than in the past. How, and why is this?

All human tissues require oxygen. This is supplied by red blood cells. The heart is responsible for pumping the blood around the body: to the lungs where the cells become saturated with oxygen, then back to the heart and then to the tissues where the oxygen is released.

During the course of a day, different parts of the body will need different amounts of oxygen: when we run, our muscles need more; when we eat, our stomachs need more. There are many very clever changes we constantly make to our circulation in order to meet these demands: the heart can beat faster or more strongly, the blood vessels can tighten up or relax.

The heart itself is made of a special type of muscle tissue which needs oxygen. This muscle tissue is contracting and relaxing all the time so its demand for oxygen is high. The oxygen comes

from blood travelling through small vessels called the *coronary arteries*.

If the oxygen supply is reduced because, for example, these vessels become narrowed or blocked, the heart muscle may not have enough to support its needs. It may become damaged and not work properly – it may die. This is what happens in a **heart attack**.

Narrowing of the arteries

Blood vessels are lined by special cells. In some places, the inside of these cells may become thickened, and fatty substances called lipids (which circulate in the blood) get deposited there.

By themselves, these deposits may narrow the blood vessels enough to threaten the oxygen supply to the tissues. Sometimes, the fatty area breaks down: the clotting mechanism in the blood responds as if this were a break in the blood vessel wall and tries to plug it.

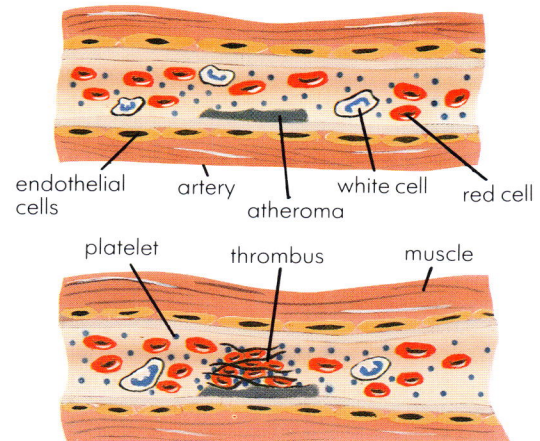

endothelial cells   artery   atheroma   white cell   red cell

platelet   thrombus   muscle

The fatty atheroma may breakdown. The blood clots because small cells called 'platelets' stick to the area, become activated and a 'thrombus' is formed, which may block the vessel.

If this happens a *'thrombus'* is formed. This may block the vessel completely or it may break off and get carried down the blood vessel and block it at a lower point.

The consequences are very serious. Heart attacks and strokes (where the thrombosis reduces the blood supply to part of the brain) kill more people in the Western world than any other disease. Why does this happen?

We don't yet know the precise reason. To help us find out, we can see how many cases occur in which types of people over what period of time. Such research has shown that we are more likely to develop fatty deposits in the blood vessels if we

- Are male
- Have relatives who have (or had) the disease
- Live in the 'developed' world
- Smoke cigarettes
- Are fatter than we should be
- Have high blood pressure
- Eat food full of saturated fats
- Take no exercise
- Do a job that puts us under a lot of pressure
- Drink too much alcohol
- Also suffer from some other disease, such as diabetes
- Have a personality that makes us angry, anxious or over-active

Some of these things – our sex, our relatives, where we were born and where we live – we cannot control. Others, such as cigarette smoking, we can. Are there any others from the list that you think we can modify? How?

Which of them do you think are due to our 'external' environment, and which due to our 'internal'?

Blood pressure

If the heart did not pump the blood under pressure, the parts farthest away would not be reached.

We can measure the blood pressure quite easily by using a pressure cuff round the arm. In some people, the pressure is higher than in others. We don't yet know precisely why this happens; we do know that changes in some of our hormones can raise our blood pressure. It may be that people with high blood pressure have some disorder in their 'internal environment' that we do not as yet understand.

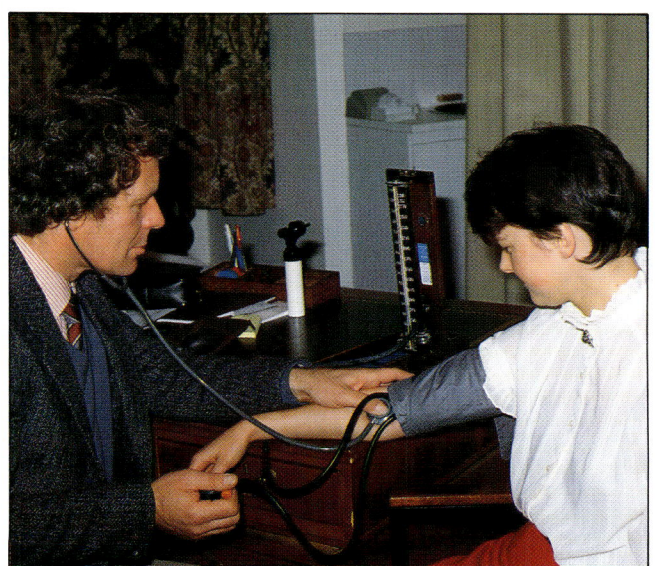

Measuring blood pressure helps us to find people at risk from heart disease.

What we do understand is how to treat it: if it is mildly raised, then reducing weight, alcohol consumption and smoking will all help. If it is moderately raised, we also need to use medicines – of which there are now many different effective ones.

We may therefore be beginning to control the ever-increasing problem of heart disease: this is one of the benefits of medical research.

NOW TRY THESE

1 Why is oxygen vital to the body?

2 Which diseases are the main killers of people in the Western world?

3 In what ways might you be able to prevent yourselves developing heart disease?

Discuss your answers.

10 Environmental and nutritional factors in disease

Industrial pollution can cause disease.

We are all affected by our external environment: what we breathe, what we eat, the substances we are in contact with during the course of our daily lives.

Many people work safely with very dangerous materials because we have discovered the precautions we must take to protect them. Chemical workers do not get poisoned, radiographers – who work with X-rays – do not get exposed to radiation.

By making our environment cleaner – for example, by reducing the amount of smoke produced by factories and homes – we have reduced the incidence of some chest diseases like *chronic bronchitis*, but not as much as we could if we *all* stopped smoking.

Can you think of any other 'external' environmental factors that might affect our health? What can we do about them?

Our defence system

Our 'internal' environment – as we have already seen – can also affect our health. Our bodies have protective mechanisms to help us fight off anything that the body regards as foreign. The *defence system* is complicated. Different types of cells have different functions but they

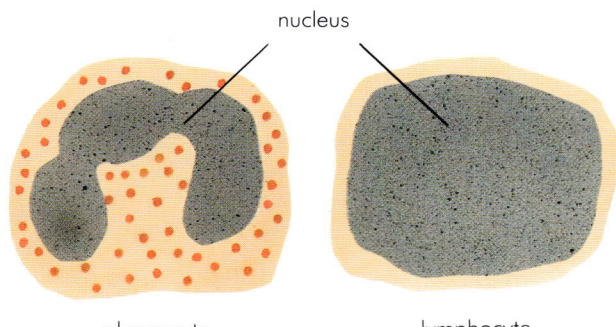

Two different types of white blood cells.
The white blood cells form the basis of our protective mechanisms: our immune defences.

all work together (the way they help fight viral infections is described on page 7).

Sometimes when our bodies are attacked by toxic substances, there are cells which respond by releasing a chemical called **histamine**. This both increases blood flow to the area and allows other cells – like **macrophages** – to escape from the blood vessels to deal with the toxic substance. This happens, for example, when we are stung by nettles.

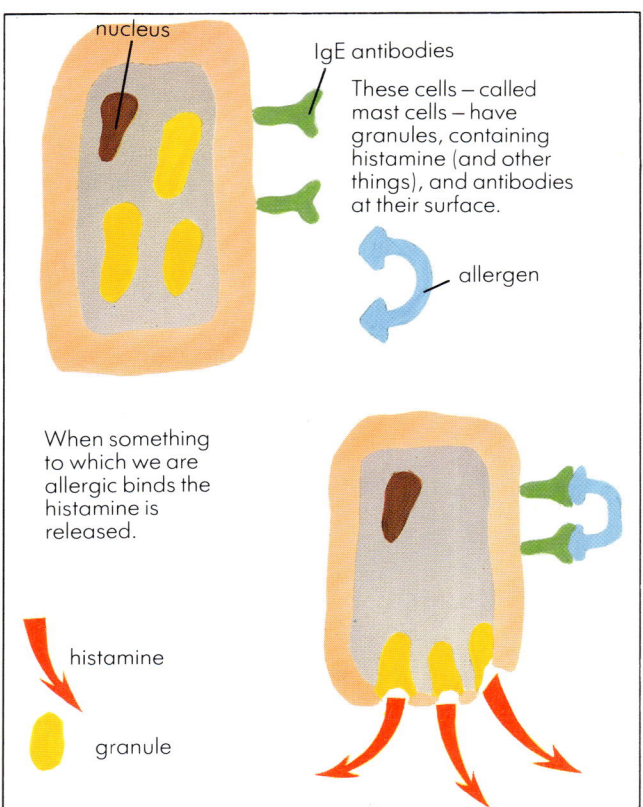

Diagram to show histamine release.

Allergy

Other cells, like **lymphocytes**, do different things. One function of lymphocytes is to produce chemicals called antibodies (page 7) which attack 'foreign' substances. There are different types of antibody. One of them called IgE can cause histamine to be released from mast cells. Sometimes we produce antibodies to common things, such as pollen, and, when we are exposed to them, we respond by producing too much histamine: this is the basis of **allergy**. Nearly 10% of the population suffer from allergic reactions: these may be thought of as disorders of the internal environment: the defences have over-reacted.

More serious over-reactions can occur if we eat something to which we are *allergic*, or get stung by something; we can produce a generalised reaction with a giant nettle rash.

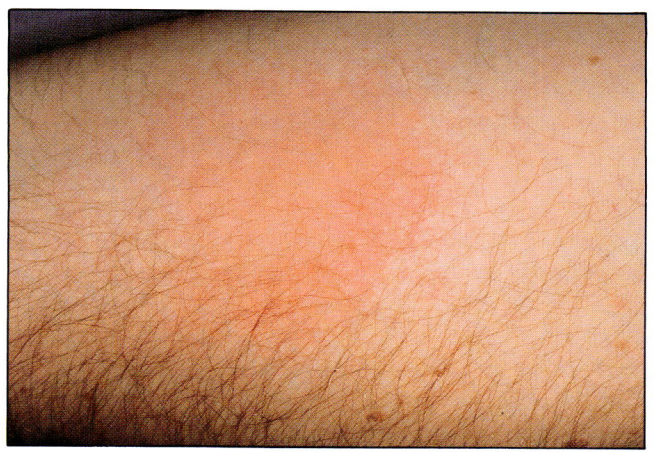

Nettle rash. Histamine is released and increases the blood flow to the area of injury, together with leakiness of the tiny vessels. This is to allow the circulating body defences to reach the site and remove the foreign material.

This over-reaction, or hypersensitivity, does not merely affect the skin: we have histamine-releasing cells in our lungs. The interaction of macrophages and antibodies and histamine, with other cells, can cause the muscles in the terminal parts of the lung – the 'bronchioles' – to tighten, and also produce excessive mucus. The airways become narrowed, and affected people find it difficult to breathe. This is **asthma**.

Two million people in the UK are affected by asthma. It kills 2 000 of them every year. What can we do?

Once the body has 'learned' that something is foreign, it is difficult to make it forget. Sometimes we can discover what the offending substance is, but often we can't. At present, we

can treat the shortness of breath by medicines; it would be better to prevent it developing. This is the aim of research.

Allergy and asthma arise because the defence system of the body over-responds. There are other diseases which arise because the defence system makes a mistake, and decides some part of ourselves is *foreign*. It then produces antibodies which set out to try to destroy that part of the body. They may attack our joints, for example, which can be very disabling. If they attack our muscles, we can become immobile.

At present, we don't know why these things happen: we have learned about the antibodies, we are learning about the people who may develop them, and about how we might treat them; but there is still a lot to learn!

Vitamin deficiencies

These may be caused by defects in our diets or by defects in the way we deal with the vitamins once we have them.

Vitamin C is a chemical which is essential for the proper formation of skin and the absorption of iron. It is found in fresh citrus fruits. Deficiency of these in the diet can cause illness – no longer common in this country, but in poorer countries becoming more so.

Vitamin D is necessary for the proper development of bones. It is made in the liver and kidney. It is produced with the help of sunlight on our skin.

With an adequate diet and enough sunlight, we produce enough vitamin D, and therefore strong bones. If children are deficient, they develop deformed joints; adults develop painful bones. Which people do you think might become deficient?

As with any other vitamin deficiencies, we can correct this by providing supplements. You might find it interesting to discover which foods contain which of the vitamins we need.

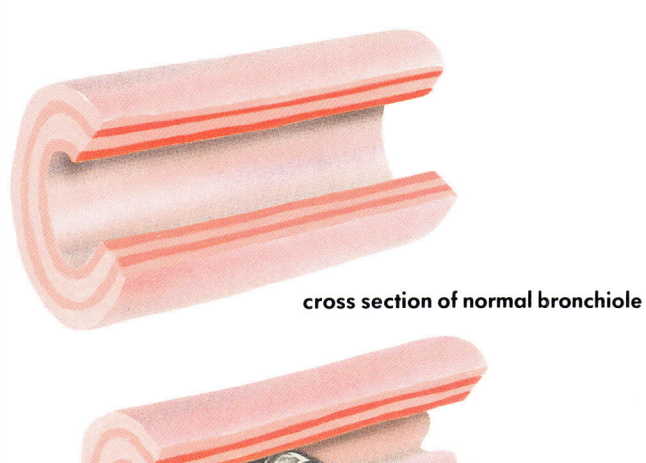

cross section of normal bronchiole

cross section of bronchiole with blocked airway – as occurs in asthma

NOW TRY THESE

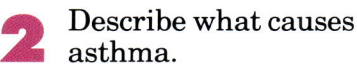

1 Name one of the beneficial effects of sunlight.

2 Describe what causes asthma.

3 Do you think any people in this country might be short of vitamins? Why?

Preventing the illegal importation of infected animals, and strict quarantine of legally imported animals, stops the disease. (Crown copyright reserved)

'Prevention is better than cure.' If we can prevent a person contracting or developing an illness, it's better than providing treatment once they've fallen ill.

Passive prevention

The best prevention is by preventing exposure: if you're not in contact with the disease, you can't catch it. This is how strict quarantine laws keep Britain free from *rabies*, which is a disease caused by a virus and spread by the bite of an infected animal.

In order to prevent contact with diseases, we need to know how they are spread. This is established by medical researchers called **epidemiologists** who study which people get particular diseases and in which countries: putting together all the information about all the cases of a particular illness gives clues as to how the disease may be spread. By studying, early in this century, the way in which the Black Plague spread, it was possible to establish that the disease came from rats to men by way of fleas. Killing the rats and the fleas removed the disease from Europe.

Many other diseases have been prevented in similar ways. Recently, an outbreak of

Legionnaires' Disease – a type of pneumonia caused by a bacterium called *Legionella* – occurred in Kingston-upon-Thames, centred around the hospital.

Work in America had already shown that the bacterium flourished in static water supplies such as in air-conditioning units, and was spread in tiny droplets. The epidemiologists in Kingston were able to trace the source to a cooling tower and a separate water supply. Effective cleansing and purification prevented further cases, since there was no further exposure. This might be called **passive prevention**: the body takes no action.

The Legionella bacterium develops in the static water, and is carried through the air in droplets.

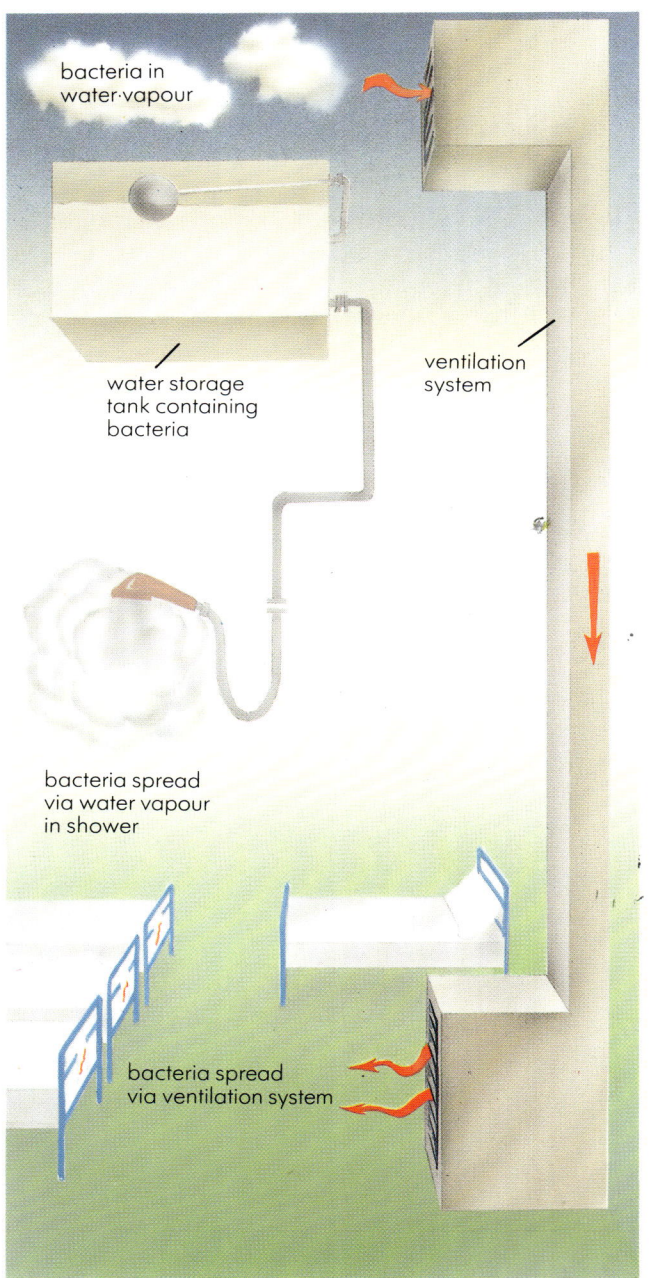

bacteria in water-vapour

water storage tank containing bacteria

ventilation system

bacteria spread via water vapour in shower

bacteria spread via ventilation system

Active prevention

Since we don't live in sterile glass bubbles, we can't prevent exposure to all diseases – but we can prevent them developing after we've been exposed to them by using the body's own defences. This depends on the activation of the immune defences.

The defence system consists of a number of different white blood cells – lymphocytes – which attack viruses in a number of ways (by producing antibodies, for example), and **neutrophils** which attack bacteria – and macrophages which help to activate the other cells, together with a number of large protein molecules, which work both to attack invading cells and to call up the white blood cells to help in the attack.

Immunisation

The baby's defence system is immature . . .

. . . when the lymphocytes are exposed to the vaccine they respond and produce more cells – called *memory* cells – which remember the virus (the primary response)

If the infection is encountered again, the memory cells respond very quickly (the secondary response) and overwhelm the virus (or bacteria) that has caused the infection – the baby is *immune*

The body attacks much more quickly if it has met the invading cell before. This is why immunisation prevents disease. It involves exposing the body to a harmless substance which looks sufficiently like the real thing to stimulate the defences, but which does not cause the illness.

Medical research has enabled the development of different types of vaccine active against a number of diseases: for example, oral polio vaccine (Wellcome Laboratories) consists of an **attenuated** virus – that is one that is sufficiently weak not to cause disease. The use of polio vaccine has dramatically reduced the incidence of polio in the developed world.

The vaccine against cholera consists of killed bacteria. Since they are dead they cannot cause infection, but they do stimulate the body's defence mechanisms.

Similar vaccines exist for other diseases, such as German measles (rubella) and tetanus. As a result many cases of disease have been prevented, and at least one killer disease (small-pox) has been wiped out. Active medical research is aimed at producing vaccines against other diseases, such as AIDS.

NOW TRY THESE

1 What is meant by the body's 'defence systems'?

2 How does immunisation prevent us getting diseases?

Some people are more at risk of developing certain illnesses than the rest of us. Identifying these groups of people at an early stage of the disease means treatment can be offered before too much damage has been done. There are a number of ways to identify such 'at-risk' groups.

Screening

Screening is the process which aims to detect disease before it has produced symptoms, so that people can benefit from early treatment.

People who may be 'at risk' are tested to see if they have signs indicating a particular disease; if they have, they can be examined further to see how far the disease has developed. Often, the test detects signs indicating that the disease will develop in the future, but it is not currently present. Effective treatment may help prevent the disease occurring.

Cancer of the cervix (neck of the womb) was a common condition, but in many countries the incidence has been much reduced by mass screening.

This disease develops slowly; it takes about 10 years from the time the first changes appear in the cells to the development of a dangerous cancer. The changes can easily be seen by using the microscope to examine a number of cells scraped from the cervix – a **cervical smear**. A laser beam can be used to destroy the abnormal cells at an early stage, and thereby prevent the development of cervical cancer.

If all women at risk were screened at regular intervals, cancer of the cervix would almost certainly become a disease of the past.

In **diabetes mellitus**, the level of glucose (or sugar) in the blood is too high, either because there is not enough **insulin** (a hormone that helps the body use sugar to produce energy) or because the cells on which the insulin acts do not respond to it.

High levels of sugar are dangerous both in the short and the long term. In the long term, one of the complications may be blindness.

People with diabetes mellitus can be regularly monitored to ensure that their blood glucose level is kept as near normal as possible.

If all people 'at risk' of developing diabetes, or who have the disease, were regularly screened, then blindness due to diabetes mellitus could become a disease of the past.

Inherited diseases

How do we know who might be 'at risk'? Diabetes mellitus is a disease which, like some others, may run in families. Identifying people who may have a disease because their parents or grandparents had it, or who have a disease which they might pass on to their own children, involves medical researchers working in the field of **genetics**.

This means both seeing how a disease affects different generations of a family, and studying the cells of people in the family to see if they might get the disease. We can do this because we are all developed from cells containing *chromosomes* – each made up of many genes – which we get from our parents.

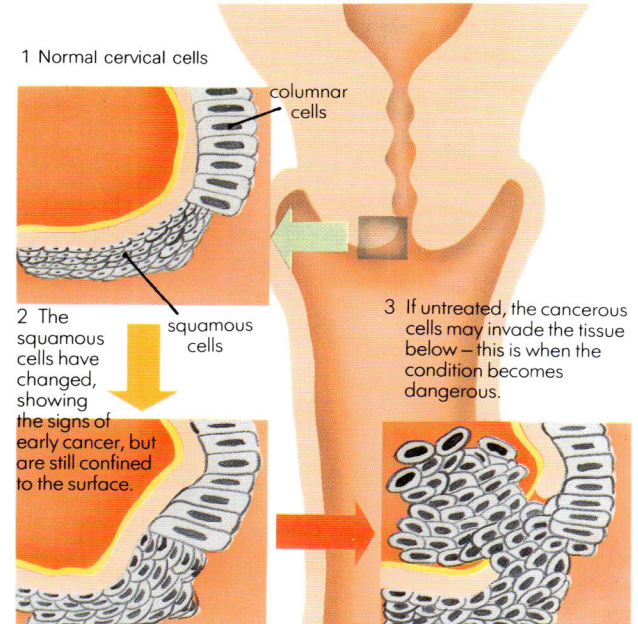

1 Normal cervical cells

columnar cells

squamous cells

2 The squamous cells have changed, showing the signs of early cancer, but are still confined to the surface.

3 If untreated, the cancerous cells may invade the tissue below – this is when the condition becomes dangerous.

Part of the female reproductive system, showing a close-up view of cancer of the cervix.

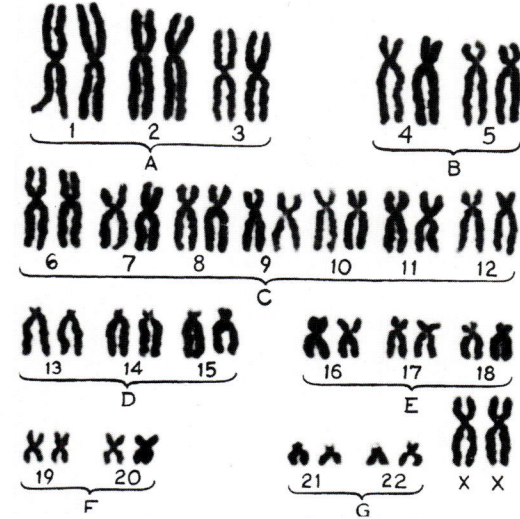

Normal female chromosomes (ie with two Xs). We get one sex-determining chromosomes from each of our parents.

Each person has 22 pairs of chromosomes together with two chromosomes which determine our sex. Females have 2 X chromosomes and males an X and a Y. This genetic material determines not only what we look like, but also to a large extent the way we develop, and the diseases we might contract. Half the chromosomes come from each parent, with the egg providing the X and the sperm either an X or a Y. Once the two have joined, the resulting cell has the total of 46 chromosomes including the sex-determining chromosomes (ie 44 chromosomes + 2 Xs (or an X and a Y)).

In **Down's Syndrome**, instead of 46 chromosomes there are 47 – ie an extra number 21. This arises either because there are problems in the development of the egg – which happens more frequently as the mother gets older – or because one of the parents has their number 21 stuck onto another chromosome. The parent will be normal but they may pass on the abnormal chromosome to an offspring, and produce a child with Down's Syndrome.

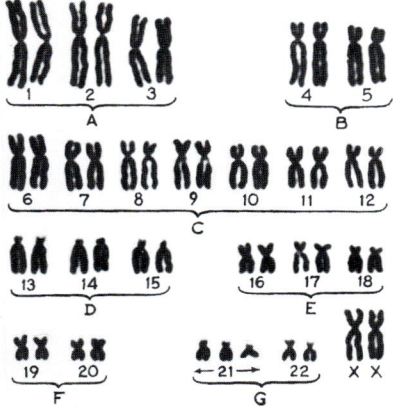

The chromosomes of a female with Down's Syndrome. There are three number 21s.

A young girl with Down's Syndrome.

We can look at the chromosomes of parents of children with Down's Syndrome, and find those with an abnormal chromosome. In any subsequent pregnancy or with any other pregnant women thought to be 'at risk', a small sample of the fluid surrounding the developing baby can be withdrawn (this technique is called *amniocentesis*). The cells in the fluid can be grown and examined to see if the foetus has the disease. If it has, then the parents may choose to have the pregnancy ended; however, many people believe it wrong to end pregnancies.

This is a technique now commonly used to detect problems in the developing foetus which may be at risk from a number of diseases. There are many other diseases, however, where more work is needed to understand the precise nature of the genetic problem.

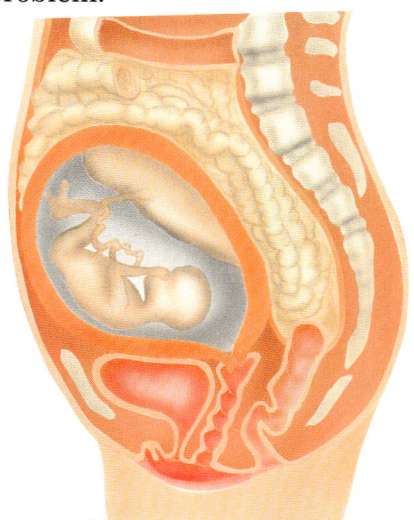

Using ultrasound to get an accurate picture of the location of the baby, we can quite safely draw off some fluid from around it. The fluid contains cells which have the baby's chromosomes, which can be cultured and tested.

NOW TRY THESE

1 What are inherited diseases, and can they be prevented?

2 Which parent's chromosomes determine the sex of the baby, and why?

3 What is the function of insulin in the body?

4 What are the pros and cons of being able to detect genetic disorders before the child is born?

13 Intervening in disease

Investigating

All of us are covered by skin: none of us can see through it. How do we know what is happening inside somebody who is ill? Medical research has learned to use discoveries made by other researchers to help in the investigation of sick people.

X-rays, like light waves, are part of a spectrum of electromagnetic waves.

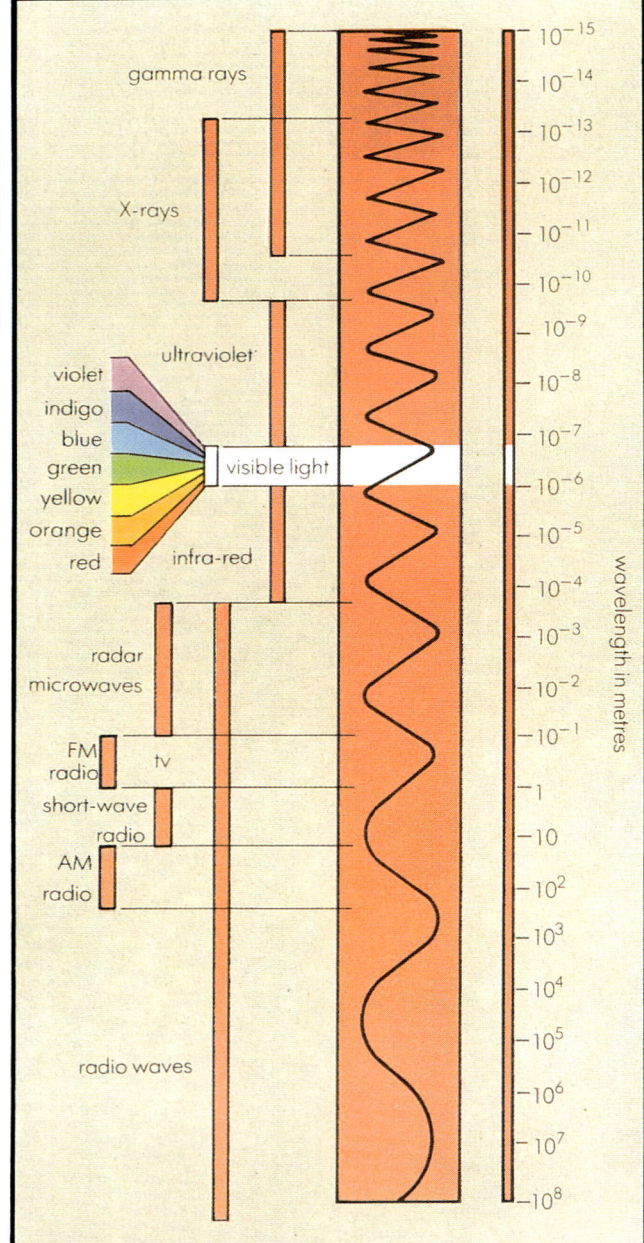

The electromagnetic spectrum.

The difference between light waves and X-rays is that X-rays can penetrate substances that light waves can't. These rays were first discovered by a physicist named Röntgen in 1895. They were soon applied to medicine. Bones are more solid than skin, and show up white on photographic film, while air appears black.

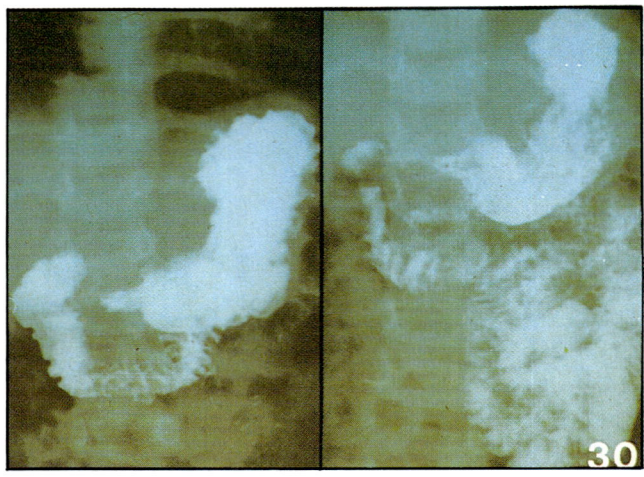

The stomach is filled with barium sulphate so that we can see its outline. Shortly after, the barium moves further down the gut.

If something – like a tumour – develops in the lung, the X-ray may show it. How do we see if a tumour has developed in other deeper areas, such as the bowel? We can use an opaque dye to show in 'outline' or 'shadow' what we can't see directly. Using liquids containing substances that appear very white on X-rays – like barium sulphate, which is harmless – we can fill the stomach or bowel, and any abnormality will be clearly seen.

Some parts of the body, like the brain, are made of tissues much less dense than bone, and X-rays pass straight through. We can 'see' these structures by linking the X-ray machine to a computer.

The X-ray machine takes many pictures. The computer analyses the results and helps to produce the picture: this is computer-aided tomography or CAT scanning. Using it, we can see clearly structures that were invisible before.

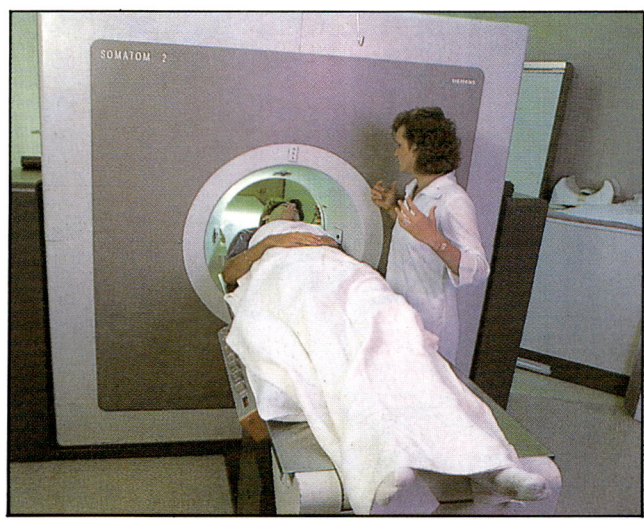

A person undergoing a CAT scan (computer aided tomography).

Ultrasound image of a human foetus in the womb, after seven months development, showing the face and shoulders in profile. Measurements from such photographs tell us how the baby is developing.

Ultrasound

Although the X-rays we use are relatively harmless to us, they can be harmful to the developing baby. We can use ultrasonic sound waves (**ultrasound**) – which are harmless to everything – to examine any structure that has different densities. The technique involves sending out the waves and measuring the time it takes for the echoes to return. Each reflection is represented by a dot on the screen and a picture of the structure is built.

This enables us to monitor the growth of babies before they are born. Similarly, we can investigate problems in the kidneys or the liver.

Laboratory tests

X-rays and ultrasound look from the outside in. Nuclear medicine and other methods look from the inside out. The most accurate information of all is obtained by taking samples such as blood from the body and subjecting them to analysis in the laboratory. Improvements in laboratory techniques mean that we can now look at cells magnified hundreds of thousands of times in order to:

a) identify single genes in individual chromosomes

b) monitor a person's response to treatment minute by minute

c) detect small amounts of toxins or poisons.

These advances, together with many others, mean that many of us are much healthier than our ancestors were.

Nuclear medicine

Radioactive isotopes are forms of elements that are unstable. They become stable by giving off radiation.

Using short-lived radioactive substances, such as radioactive iodine, we can take pictures of some inner organs of the body – like the thyroid, which concentrates iodine.

NOW TRY THESE

1 What is the difference between X-rays and light waves?

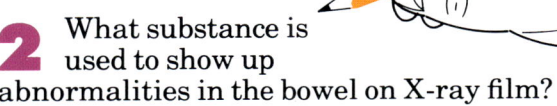

2 What substance is used to show up abnormalities in the bowel on X-ray film?

3 What are radioactive isotopes? How are they useful to doctors?

4 Name some other diagnostic tests that are available to doctors.

27

Knowing the reasons why things happen may help us to put up with whatever discomfort they cause, but it does not necessarily improve our quality of life. What have we gained from medical research?

For all of us, there is an improved quality of life with less ill-health and greater life expectancy. In the UK as a result of vaccination, good nutrition and prompt health care, the life expectancy is much greater than in underdeveloped countries and the infant mortality rate is much lower.

If we fall ill, we have more chance of effective treatment: for example, if we have pains in the chest when we exercise, because our coronary arteries are narrowed, we can be investigated and treated before we have a heart attack.

The coronary arteries themselves can be examined using X-rays and a dye injected through a tiny tube placed in the artery. If there is a point where the artery has narrowed, it may be possible to make it wider by blowing up a tiny balloon in the artery.

If this is not possible, the arteries can be replaced using veins from our legs. We can do this because we have developed machines to take over the function of the heart and lungs – the pumping and oxygenation of the blood – while the heart is stopped.

Those of us unlucky enough to have kidney disease (which used always to be fatal) can now be saved as a result of medical research: **dialysis** machines can take over the function of the kidneys until a suitable donor kidney can be transplanted.

During dialysis, waste products can be removed from the blood by filtration using a machine such as this, which does the work of the kidneys.

Transplant operations are becoming more and more common now and a greater degree of success is attainable, because
a) laboratory tests to identify a good 'match' between the donor and the recipient are becoming more refined, and b) control of the normal body response – rejection of the transplanted organ as 'foreign' – is more easily achieved using modern medicines.

In many other areas great advances have helped ease suffering: as a result of laboratory techniques, previously infertile couples can now have children.

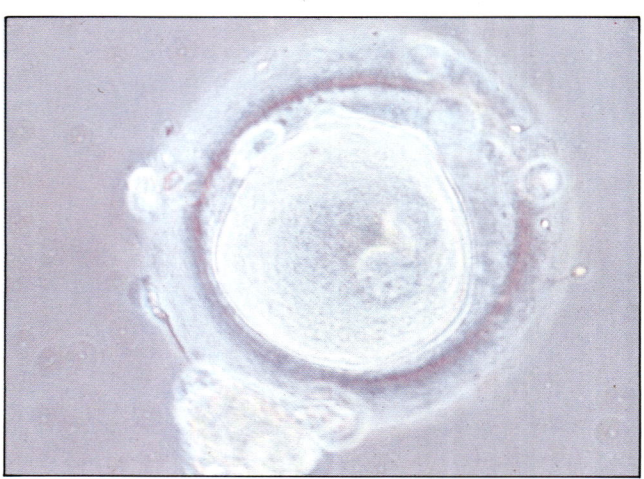

In vitro *fertilisation: by fertilising the egg in the laboratory and then replacing it into the womb, the woman can carry through a normal pregnancy and produce a normal child.*

Throughout the book, there are examples of illnesses that have been cured, eased or eradicated as a result of medical research. Can you find them? Can you now answer the questions asked at the beginning?

NOW TRY THESE

1 Which factors resulting from medical research have improved the quality of life for all of us in the UK?

2 Transplant operations cost a lot of money and are not always successful. Do you think it is worth spending money on transplants? Discuss your answer.

3 What do you understand by in vitro fertilisation?

4 Why should babies born as a result of this method not be called 'test-tube' babies? Give advantages and disadvantages.

15 Who does medical research?

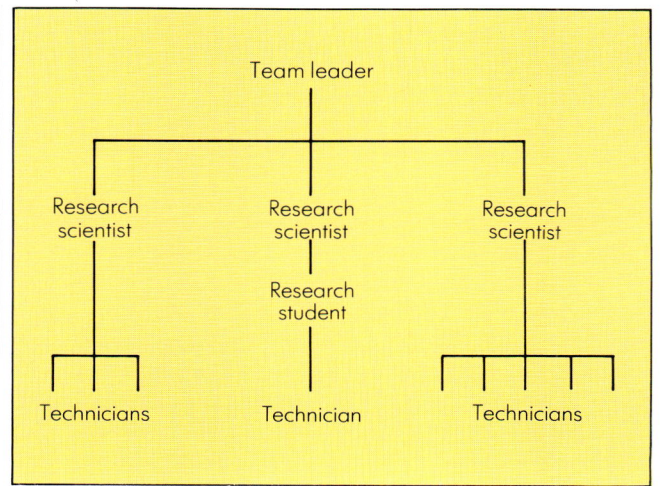

A 'research' tree.

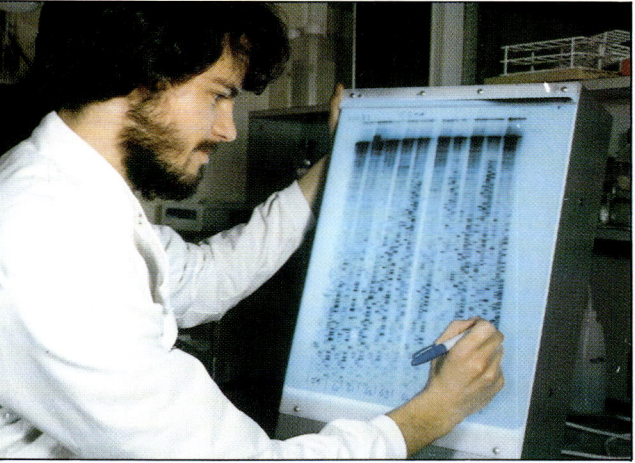

Medical research involves both individual and team work. The individual may have the idea, the team will work towards developing that idea.

On the whole, medical research is carried out by research workers working together in teams. A typical medical research team consists of a number of people with different skills, attempting to solve a specific problem: in charge will be a *team leader*.

As an expert in his subject, he helps to produce and develop ideas, and direct the work of the team of highly skilled and qualified researchers who apply their special knowledge of the general area of the problem to attempt to find a solution, and then design the experiments to test their ideas. They are helped by technicians – people skilled in laboratory techniques or in the use of instruments such as electron microscopes.

Such a team will also have the assistance of experts in other subjects, such as **statistics** – in order to check the validity of their results – and computer science, to help analyse them. Let's see how this might work in practice. Suppose we want to develop a vaccine against a viral illness such as AIDS. There are in general two different aspects to medical research: laboratory-based research and clinical research involving patients.

With a viral illness, the first step is identifying the disease. This involves *clinicians* – medical doctors working with patients – who diagnose the illness, often using laboratory tests to help them, and *epidemiologists*, who study the history and spread of disease.

Having identified the illness, we need to find the cause.

In the laboratory, samples from infected patients are studied by **virologists** – experts in the behaviour of viruses. They isolate the virus and persuade it to grow on special cells so that more is available for study.

Then microscopists can examine its structure under the microscope. The biochemists can establish its genetic component and the nature of its covering coat; the immunologists can examine the response of suitable animal hosts when exposed to it.

What is now needed is the identification or development of a harmless substance that will provoke the same immune response in the animal.

The virologists will search either for similar but harmless viruses, or for ways of rendering the virus itself harmless while not removing its ability to provoke the immune response. This might be achieved by killing the virus – by heat, for example – or by attempting to make it weaker; it will be infectious but not dangerous.

The biochemist will use experiments to break the virus into small pieces. The immunologists will test the effects of the different pieces on the immune system of the animal to find any that will provoke an immune response.

Once a safe agent has been found – either a dead virus or a weakened one or a part of one – animal studies are used to establish whether it will promote immunity. If it does and is safe, human volunteers (often the researchers themselves) are given the vaccine. If this is safe and produces antibodies, a small-scale trial can be performed, where a limited number of people – possibly those at high risk from the disease – will be treated. Only if this proves safe will the vaccine be released for general use.

You can see that such research involves hundreds of people, and is not quick, nor easy nor cheap. To develop a new medicine or vaccine costs many millions of pounds.

Is only medical research of use in medicine?

By no means: many of the advances made in medical research have been based on the results of research in pure science. Without such discoveries, we would not be able to treat many conditions. Basic scientific research is of the greatest importance, as is interaction and sharing of results between researchers working in different subjects or different places.

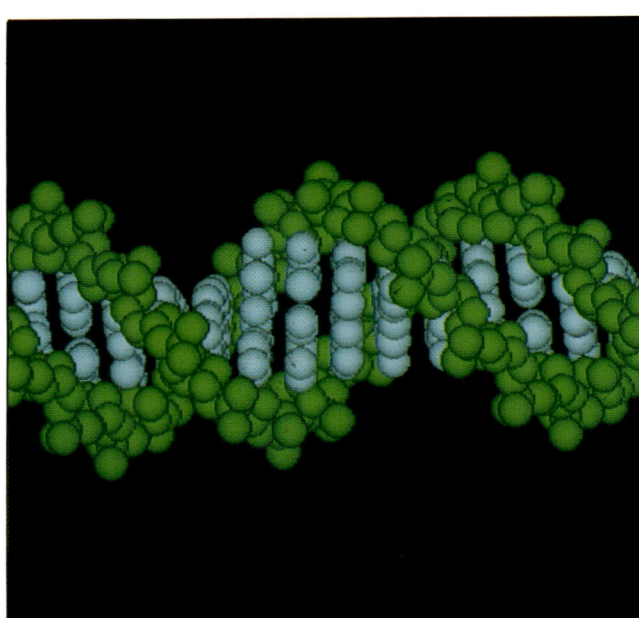

Understanding the structure of large molecules helped our knowledge of many diseases. Solving the puzzle of DNA opened the door to many other discoveries.

Where is research done in the UK?

Laboratory research is carried out in universities, in specialist research institutes like the Medical Research Council (MRC) units, hospital laboratories and the laboratories of pharmaceutical companies.

Clinical medical research is carried out wherever there are patients: hospitals are used in the initial trials of new treatments and the development of new techniques. Larger numbers involved in clinical trials or epidemiological research are gathered from patients attending family doctors' surgeries.

Who pays?

The Government, through the MRC, sponsors research costing more than £130 million every year.

Medical research trusts are organisations with large endowments – either from industry or from individuals – who use the income from their investments to sponsor research.

A number of *pharmaceutical companies* perform research in order to develop their own discoveries or to find new treatments. Pharmaceutical industries currently spend about £600 million on medical research every year.

Charitable bodies – most of whom belong to the Association of Medical Research Charities – raise money from the public to support research into particular diseases, like most of those you have read about in this book. Through granting their funds to university laboratories with a particular expertise, they help to solve some of the problems.

Medical charities and trusts spend over £100 million on research each year.

WHAT YOU CAN DO

Medical research costs £15–20 per person per year. Calculate how much you spend per year on clothes, records, magazines and sweets. How much do adults you know spend on alcohol, tobacco and entertainment?

More general questions

1 Explain in your own words some of the reasons given in the text for doing medical research.

2 Describe the research process prior to the release of a vaccine for use by the general public.

3 In general, outline the measures suggested in the text to prevent and eradicate disease.

4 Do you think the cost of medical research is justified by the result obtained in terms of reducing or eradicating disease?

Glossary

Acne A skin disease caused by blockage of small lubricating glands.

Active prevention Preventing diseases by the activation of the body's defences.

Allergy Over-reaction of the body's defences after exposure to an *antigen*.

Antibiotic(s) A chemical substance that is effective in preventing the growth of bacteria.

Antibody A chemical produced by *lymphocytes* as part of our defences. (Plural: antibodies.)

Antigen Something that stimulates the body's defence systems.

Asexual(ly) Reproduction without involvement of male and female forms.

Asthma Shortness of breath as a result of narrowing of the airways.

Attenuated Reduced in strength.

Bacterium A single-celled member of the plant family, some of which cause disease. (Plural: bacteria.)

Cataract A thickening of the lens of the eye.

Cell wall A fairly rigid structure surrounding the inside of bacteria.

Cervical smear A sample of cells taken from the cervix and examined under the microscope.

Diabetes mellitus A disease where the levels of sugar in the body are too high (*mellitus* means sweet).

Dialysis The removal of waste products from the blood by filtration through a machine.

Differentiation The production of different structures by cells as they divide.

Down's Syndrome A disorder in which there is an extra chromosome number 21.

Elephantiasis A disease caused by a parasite which blocks the drainage of fluid from the lower limbs.

Epidemic(s) An outbreak of a disease in a community at a particular time.

Epidemiologist(s) A person who studies the spread and development of diseases.

Epilepsy A disease resulting from over-active electrical signals in the brain.

Genetics The way in which we inherit our bodily characteristics from our parents.

Heart attack The death of muscle cells in the heart, usually as a result of narrowing of the arteries.

Herpes A family of viruses causing such diseases as chicken pox and cold sores.

Histamine A chemical released by certain cells in the body in response to toxic stimuli.

Host An animal in which a *parasite* exists.

Immunisation Stimulation of the immune system by the introduction of an innocuous *antigen*.

Infectious A disease which can be passed from one person to another.

Insulin A hormone normally produced by cells in the pancreas. It enables us to utilise the glucose in our bloodstream.

Louse A *parasite* which may transmit diseases.

Lymphocyte(s) One of the white blood cells. They are concerned with attacks on *viruses* and production of *antibodies*.

Macrophage(s) A white blood cell involved in many aspects of our defence systems.

Malaria An infectious disease caused by the parasite *plasmodium*, spread by the bite of a mosquito.

Micro-organism A species capable of life, being so small as to be visible only with the aid of a microscope.

Neutrophil(s) A white blood cell which attacks bacteria.

Parasite An organism which lives in, and draws nourishment from, another.

Parkinson's disease A disease of the nervous system caused by a lack of a chemical messenger in the brain.

Passive prevention Preventing diseases by not allowing exposure to them.

Penicillin An *antibiotic* which stops the development of some bacterial *cell walls*.

Phagocyte(s) A number of white blood cells, such as *macrophages*, involved in our defence systems.

Platelet A small white blood cell involved in blood clotting and parts of our defences.

Polio An *infectious* disease caused by a *virus*. It may cause paralysis, and is prevented by *immunisation*.

Ribosome(s) Intra-cellular structures necessary for the production of new proteins.

Schizophrenia A mental disorder in which people may have thoughts and feelings that seem not to be their own (Greek *schizo* = split, *phrenia* = mind).

Screening Examination of people at risk of a disease, to see if they have it.

Statistics The science of the collection and analysis of numerical facts.

Transplant An operation in which an organ is removed from one person and placed in another.

Tuberculosis An *infectious* disease caused by the *tubercle bacillus*.

Typhus A disease caused by an organism called a rickettsia, spread by the bite of a body *louse*.

Ultrasound The use of high-frequency sound waves to study internal organs or the developing foetus.

Vaccine A harmless substance (such as a modified *virus*) used to promote immunity.

Virus(es) An *infectious micro-organism* consisting of simple genetic material and a covering. Viruses are responsible for many diseases.

Index

Commissioning Editor: Dr W T Mason
Designer: Douglas Whitworth
Illustrations: Chris Feely Illustration

Acknowledgements

We would like to thank the following for supplying photographic material:

Age Concern England/Adrian Spalding
Biophoto Associates
Cancer Research Campaign
Department of Obstetrics and Gynaecology,
   University of Cambridge
Down's Syndrome Association
Feature-Pix Colour Library/J Edmonson
Leicester Biocentre
Medical Research Council
Ministry of Agriculture, Fisheries and Food
Science Photo Library/CDC, CNRI,
   Larry Mulvehill, Sheila Terry
The British Kidney Patient Association
Wellcome Institute Library, London
   (by kind permission of the Trustees of the
   Wellcome Trust 1988)
Wellcome Tropical Institute
Dr Paul Wheater